A *Golden Hands* book

THE NEW ROSE BOOK

Marshall Cavendish, London

Pictures supplied by:
Heather Angel 73(T)
D. C. Arminson 80, 86
Dr. P. Becker 71 (T&C)
Michael Boys 64
R. J. Corbin 12 (BL), 65, 66, 67, 68, 69, 70,
72 (BR), 75, 76, 77, 78 (B), 81, 82, 83, 86, 88,
89
J. K. B. Cowley 83
Ernest Crowson 15-63 *passim*
J. E. Drummond 79 (TL)
Faulkner/Marks 74
Valerie Finnis 6 (BL), 7, 78 (T)
J. W. T. Howden 73 (B), 83
Peter Hunt 15-63 *passim*
G. E. Hyde 72 (TR)
John Ledger 94
Patrick Matthews 15-63 *passim*, 90, 92
L. Hugh Newman 71 (B), 72 (TL)
Harry Smith 5, 6 (T&BR), 8, 9, 10, 11,
12 (T, C, BR), 79, 91, 93
Colin Watmough 13

T=top, C=centre, B=bottom
L=left, R=right

Published by Marshall Cavendish Publications Limited,
58, Old Compton Street,
London, W1V 5PA.

© Marshall Cavendish Ltd, 1968, 1969, 1970, 1973
58, Old Compton Street,
London, W1V 5PA.

This material first published by Marshall Cavendish Limited in
The Encyclopedia of Gardening and *150 of the World's Most Beautiful Roses*.

This volume first printed in 1974.

Printed by Colour Reproductions Limited, Billericay, Essex.
and Sir Joseph Causton & Sons Ltd, London and Eastleigh.

ISBN 0 85685 054 3

This edition is not to be sold in the United States of America, Canada or
the Philippines.

About this book . . .

Here's what every rose gardener should know! A complete, concise, up-to-date guide to caring for every type of rose, including identifying, selecting and buying, planting, pest control, and exhibiting.

For inspiration, there's a lengthy pictorial dictionary of the world's most beautiful roses – glowing full-colour plates plus a description of each rose, its growing habits and parentage.

Once you have chosen your favourite varieties, you'll need tips on arranging them successfully in a landscape. This book not only gives helpful advice on situating, combining colours and types, and choosing borders, but it shows several lovely gardens as well.

And finally is a month-by-month gardening calendar with tasks and suggestions for every time of the year. With this compact volume, no rose lover need ever be idle. For when you are not busy out in the garden following the thorough yet easily understood instructions of experts, you can simply thumb through the hundreds of colour pictures and conjure up visions for the spring.

Contents

The World's Roses

Almost no garden subject has been written about at greater length, or with more enthusiasm, than roses and their cultivation. Nevertheless, there is plenty that can be said on the matter, and the fact that roses grow easily in most parts of Britain only makes the keen gardener more than ever determined to think of everything in order to cultivate the flower to its greatest perfection.

Certainly roses will repay your attention. Whether they are grown on a fairly large scale, as, for example in the Italian rose garden at Trentham, Staffordshire, or in smaller groups in the home garden, roses provide tremendous pleasure at a reasonably small cost and minimal effort.

In an article which concentrates on the technical side of the subject it would be wrong to forget entirely the historical and romantic associations of the flower. Chaucer's *Romaunt of the Rose*, with its associations of courtly love, and the Scene in the Temple Garden, London, in Act II of Shakespeare's *King Henry VI, Part 1*, when the rival factions in the 'Wars of the Roses' plucked the red or the white rose, are just two examples of how the rose from the earliest times has come to symbolise the deepest of feelings.

Modern roses fall mainly into the following groups: hybrid tea, floribunda, standard, miniature, shrub, and rambling and climbing.

Hybrid tea These include the large flowered, shapely bedding and exhibition roses, many with a strong fragrance. The group merges the few remaining hybrid perpetuals in general cultivation and what used to be known as 'Pernetianas', representing all the original pure yellow, orange, flame and bicolor varieties. The first hybrid tea varieties were obtained crossing the hybrid perpetuals with the tea-scented roses.

Floribunda These include all the original hybrid polyanthas evolved by the rose breeder Svend Poulsen of Denmark. He crossed poly-pompoms with hybrid teas, and all the many-flowered roses (other than the poly-pompons), the climbing and rambling groups and the Pemberton, so-called 'hybrid musks'. The term 'hybrid polyantha' was discontinued soon after the Second World War, because varieties were being added to the group each year with little or no true polyantha 'blood', resulting from crossing hybrid teas with various groups of shrub roses.

Standard roses Hybrid tea and floribunda varieties may be obtained budded on 3½-foot stems (full standard), or stems 2 feet 3 inches tall (half standard). These forms are useful to provide an extra dimension where beds of bush roses might be too flat. They also enable the flowers to be admired at eye level.

Several modifications in cultivation are advisable to obtain the best results. Planting should be shallow, the top roots being covered with not more than 3 inches of soil. Staking is essential and a stout oak stake should be driven home before the roots are covered. It should be long enough to reach well up into the head of the standard to give effective support, and ties must be durable—old rubber-insulated electrical cable is excellent. Pruning must be rather lighter than for the same variety in bush form. A large symmetrical head is the objective and thinning, by cutting out the weaker growth, will be desirable. Suckers appearing on the stem below the head must be pulled off while small, and a watch kept for any springing from the root system. Insecurely staked standard roses will often throw many suckers.

Weeping standards budded on 5-foot to 6-foot stems are still in demand for planting as isolated specimens on lawns. The old wichuraiana ramblers 'Dorothy Perkins', 'Excelsa' and 'François Juranville' are among the most popular.

Fifty first-class hybrid tea roses

Name	Habit of growth	Colour	Fragrance	Name	Habit of growth	Colour	Fragrance
Anne Watkins*	T/U	Apricot, shading to cream	S	Mischief*	T/B	Rich coral-salmon	S
Beauté	M	Light orange and apricot	S	Miss Ireland*	M	Orange-salmon, reverse peach	S
Belle Blonde	M/B	Deep tawny gold	M	Mme L. Laperrière	D	Dark crimson	M
Blue Moon	M	Lavender-mauve	R	Mojave*	T/U	Burnt orange and flame	S
Buccaneer*	T/U	Rich golden-yellow	S	Montezuma	T/B	Rich reddish-salmon	S
Caramba*	M/U	Crimson, with silver reverse	S	My Choice	M	Pale carmine-pink, reverse buff-yellow	R
Chrysler Imperial	M/U	Dark velvety crimson	R	Peace*	T/B	Light yellow, edged pink	S
Diorama*	M/B	Apricot yellow, flushed pink	M	Perfecta	T/U	Cream, shaded rosy red	S
Doreen*	M/B	Chrome-yellow, shaded orange	M	Piccadilly*	M/B	Scarlet, reverse yellow	S
Dorothy Peach*	M	Golden-yellow, shaded peach	S	Pink Favourite*	T/B	Deep rose-pink	S
Eden Rose*	T	Rose-madder, paler reverse	R	Prima Ballerina*	T/U	Deep carmine-rose	R
Ena Harkness*	M/B	Velvety scarlet-crimson	R	Rose Gaujard*	T/B	White, shaded carmine-red	S
Ernest H. Morse*	M/U	Rich turkey-red	R	Sarah Arnot	T	Deep rosy-pink	S
Fragrant Cloud*	M/B	Scarlet changing crimson-lake	R	Signora*	T	Flame, pink and orange shades	M
Gail Borden*	T/B	Peach and salmon, shaded gold	S	Silver Lining	M/U	Silvery rose, paler reverse	M
Gold Crown	T/U	Deep gold, shaded red	M	Spek's Yellow*	T/U	Rich golden-yellow	S
Grand'mère Jenny*	T/U	Light yellow and peach-pink	S	Stella	M/B	Carmine-pink, shading to white	S
Grandpa Dickson*	T/U	Lemon yellow, paling to cream	S	Sterling Silver	M/U	Lavender-mauve, shaded silver	R
Helen Traubel*	T	Pink and apricot blend	M	Summer Sunshine	T	Intense golden-yellow	S
Josephine Bruce	M/S	Dark velvety crimson	R	Super Star*	T	Light pure vermilion	M
Lady Belper	M	Light orange	M	Sutter's Gold*	T	Orange-yellow, shaded pink and red	R
La Jolla	M	Pink, cream and gold blend	S	Tzigane	M	Scarlet, reverse chrome-yellow	M
Lucy Cramphorn*	T/B	Geranium-red	S	Virgo	T/U	White, tinted pale pink	S
Margaret*	M/B	China-pink, paler reverse	M	Wendy Cussons*	M/B	Rich cerise	R
McGredy's Yellow*	M/U	Light yellow without shading	S	Westminster	T	Cherry-red, reverse gold	M

Key *Habit of growth* T=tall   U=upright   M=medium   B=branching   D=dwarf   S=spreading
Fragrance S=slight   M=moderate   R=rich   *Exceptionally good in autumn

Fifty first-class floribunda roses (See key, page 4)

Name	Habit of growth	Colour	Name	habit of growth	Colour
Allgold	D	Rich golden-yellow	Lilac Charm	D/B	Silvery lilac, single flower
Anna Wheatcroft	M	Light vermilion	Lilli Marlene	M	Scarlet-crimson
Arabian Nights	T	Deep salmon-red	Lucky Charm	M	Yellow, pink and red
Arthur Bell	T/U	Deep golden yellow, paling to cream	Manx Queen	M	Orange-yellow shaded pink
Chanelle	M	Peach and buff	Masquerade	M	Yellow, changing to pink and red
Circus	M	Yellow, pink and red	Meteor	D	Orange-scarlet
Copper Delight	D	Bronze-yellow	Orangeade	M	Orange-vermilion
Daily Sketch	T	Pink and cream	Orange Sensation	M	Vermilion-scarlet
Dearest	T	Coral-rose	Paddy McGredy	D/B	Deep carmine-pink
Dorothy Wheatcroft	T	Bright orange-scarlet	Paprika	M	Bright turkey-red
Elizabeth of Glamis	M	Light salmon	Pernille Poulsen	D/B	Salmon-pink, fading lighter
Elysium	T	Pale rose, shaded salmon	Pink Parfait	M	Pastel shades of pink and cream
Evelyn Fison	M	Bright scarlet	Queen Elizabeth	T/U	Rose-pink
Europeana	M	Deep blood-red to crimson	Red Dandy	M	Scarlet-crimson, large flowers
Faust	T	Yellow shaded pink	Red Favourite	D	Dark crimson
Fervid	T	Bright poppy red	Rumba	M	Orange-yellow, edged scarlet
Frensham	T	Scarlet-crimson	Ruth Leuwerik	D	Bright scarlet shaded crimson
Golden Slippers	D	Orange and yellow shades	Scented Air	T/B	Rich salmon-pink
Golden Treasure	M/B	Deep yellow, non-fading	Shepherd's Delight	T/U	Scarlet, flame and orange
Goldgleam	M/B	Canary yellow, unfading	Sweet Repose	T	Soft pink shaded apricot
Gold Marie	T/S	Deep tawny gold, tinged red	Tambourine	T/U	Cherry-red, reverse orange-yellow
Highlight	T	Orange-scarlet	Toni Lander	M/U	Coppery salmon-red
Iceberg	T	White flushed pink	Vera Dalton	M	Medium rose-pink
Joyfulness	M	Apricot shaded pink	Violet Carson	M	Peach-pink, reverse silvery pink
Korona	T/U	Orange-scarlet, fading deep salmon	Woburn Abbey	T	Tangerine-orange and yellow

Both Hybrid Tea and Floribunda Roses
may be obtained budded on to standards.
In addition to being decorative
they are useful for varying the interest
of a rose garden.
1 A weeping standard, graceful
and delicate.
2 Rose 'Prestige' as a standard.

They may be allowed to form natural
bouquets or the growths may be secured
to wire umbrella trainers. The new canes
produced after flowering are retained for
next season's flowering, and wood which
has flowered is cut out in the autumn.
There are also many hybrid wichuraianas and modern recurrent-flowering
climbers which will make large heads
when budded on a 6-foot briar stem. These
have stiffer growth than the true

care should be taken to provide a deep pocket filled with rich soil, and water copiously in dry weather. Similarly, any window-boxes or stone troughs in which they may be planted should be deep and well drained, and they should never be allowed to dry out.

Propagation may be either by cuttings or by budding on to small rootstocks. The advantage of cuttings is that the dwarf habit of growth is retained, whereas growth may become more vigorous on rootstocks, and there is always the risk of suckers developing.

A few of the best varieties are given below under two headings, according to whether growth is very dwarf or somewhat taller.

Very dwarf

Colibri Orange-yellow, flushed pink.
Perla de Alcanada Carmine.
Perla de Montserrat Light Pink.
Pour Toi Creamy-white.
Presumida Orange-yellow in the centre, paling to cream.
Robin Cherry Red.
Simple Simon Deep Pink.
Sweet Fairy Lilac pink.
Yellow Doll Yellow, paling to cream.

Somewhat taller

Baby Gold Star Deep yellow.
Baby Masquerade Yellow, pink and red.
Cinderella Blush pink to white.
Coralin Bright salmon-red.
Easter Morning Pale yellow buds, opening cream.
Eleanor Coral pink.
Little Flirt Flame red, with pale yellow reverse.
New Penny Salmon pink to coral.
Red Imp Deep crimson.
Rosina Rich golden yellow.
Scarlet Gem Bright orange-scarlet.

Miniature roses are not house plants. While they will tolerate the dry atmosphere of living rooms for a time, they should be brought into the house only when in flower and kept well watered. As soon as the flowers are past their best the pots should be sunk outside up to their rims in soil, top-dressed with moist granulated peat and watered with a little weak fertiliser. They should provide a further crop or even two later in the season if they are looked after.

The old shrub roses It is uncertain how these roses began to be propagated, but it is believed that four species, *R. gallica, R. phoenicea, R. moschata* and *R. canina,* all natives of the Mediterranean region interbred and their progeny eventually became the popular roses of the nineteenth century.

R. gallica, said to have been a religious emblem of the Medes and Persians in the twelfth century BC, is a small, compact, upright bush with tiny thorns and a few prickles, neatly toothed and pointed leaves and light crimson flowers

weeping standard, so the effect is not as graceful, and the growth needs to be tied down to a wire trainer or some other device, such as a hoop. Although not as attractive as individual specimens as the true weeping standards, these can make a striking display of colour, often for a longer period than the three or four weeks of the true weepers. Varieties such as 'Dr W. Van Fleet' and its recurrent sport, 'New Dawn', flesh pink; 'Albertine', coppery-pink; 'Danse du Feu', orange-scarlet; 'Paul's Scarlet Climber'; 'Dortmund', crimson, with a white eye, single; and 'Parkdirektor Riggers', blood red, semi-double; are in this category.

Miniature roses These delightful roses may be regarded as a self-contained group, partly because they lend themselves to planting where there would not

Miniature Roses need all the attention afforded to ordinary Roses, but are useful for cultivating in places where Roses would not normally be grown.
1 'Baby Masquerade'.
2 'Red Imp'.
3 'Pixie'.

be facilities for planting other groups of roses. Thus, they will fit into deep stone troughs or sink gardens, window-boxes, tubs or miniature gardens of their own, with tiny beds and grass paths to scale. They are also sometimes used for planting on rock gardens and in pots. However, a word of warning is necessary. These are true roses and, as such, they need a deep, cool root run, with ample moisture, to give of their best. Therefore, when planting them on rock gardens, followed by small rounded hips. *R. phoenicea* is a lax shrub with long shoots, few prickles, small leaves, bearing tiny white or creamy flowers in bunches and small hips. It is not reliably hardy in Britain. *R. moschata,* the musk rose, has similar botanical characters to *R. phoenicea. R. canina,* the dog briar, is an arching shrub with large prickles, neat greyish leaves, pink flowers and oval hips.

Three of the species flower around midsummer. The exception is *R. moschata,* which flowers from August onwards. The resulting hybrids which bear flowers singly or in branching sprays fall into several distinct classes described below.

Gallica Mostly forms and close hybrids of *R. gallica,* usually compact, upright bushes with neat, pointed leaves, flowers semi-double or very double, with petals arranged into sections, 'quartered', often overlapping or tucked into the receptacle in the centre, 'button-eyed'; colours blush white, pink, light crimson, mauve, purplish crimson and maroon. Tiny thorns, few prickles, rounded hips.

Examples include *R. gallica officinalis,* said to have been brought from Damascus by the crusaders and hence known as the 'Red Damask' (but it should not be confused with the Damask type), 'Red Rose of Lancaster', 'Apothecary's Rose', 'Rose of Provins'. The last named is derived from the French in connection with the production of rose petal conserves, to which this rose is specially suited as its dried petals long retain their fragrance. Provins is a small town in northern central France, an agricultural centre noted for its roses. The industry of producing rose petal conserves was carried on in France and also in England. The flowers are large and open, loosely semi-double, showing stamens, light crimson. *R. gallica versicolor,* 'Rosa Mundi', a sport of the above, first recorded in the sixteenth century. The petals are striped and splashed with palest pink. Often confused with 'York and Lancaster' (see under *R. damascena*).

Other varieties, which are probably very old, include 'Conditorum', semi-double flowers, rich magenta-crimson, flushed and veined with purple, showing stamens. It is said to have been used in Hungary for the making of attar of roses and for preserving. 'Tuscany' or 'Old Velvet Rose', many petals opening flat, showing stamens, darkest maroon-crimson. 'Sissinghurst Castle', semi-double, showing stamens, petals plum-coloured, with magenta-crimson edges and flecked with the same tint.

Damask R. gallica × *R. phoenicea* (the type is named after the city of Damascus). Spindly erect or lax shrubs, thorny and prickly, leaves mostly soft and downy, small and rounded, long narrow hips, flowers mostly semi-double, pink.

Examples include *R. damascena tri-*

Rosa gallica versicolor, 'Rosa mundi', has been grown since the sixteenth century when it was first recorded.

gintipetala, soft pink, semi-double, showing stamens, leaves pale green. Forms the main plantings at Kazanlik, Bulgaria, and is planted there and elsewhere for the extraction of rose water and attar of roses. *R. damascena versicolor,* 'York and Lancaster', known before 1629, flowers pink or white or parti-coloured (not striped and splashed as in *R. gallica versicolor);* perhaps a sport of, or closely related to, *R. d. trigintipetala.* 'Celsiana', known before 1750, pale downy leaves, large loosely semi-double flowers, blush pink, showing stamens. 'Petite Lisette', recorded 1817, downy greyish foliage, flowers double, blush pink, each with 'button eye'.

Alba R. damascena × *R. canina.* Inheriting the strong growth, sparse but large prickles, greyish leaves and oval hips of *R. canina,* to which *R. damascena* brought double flowers, white or pink.

Examples include *R. alba semi-plena,* 'White Rose of York', seven-foot stems, few big prickles, hard greyish leaves, semi-double, pure white flowers, showing stamens, oval hips. Used as surrounding hedges for the Damask rose fields at Kazanlik; and yields an inferior essence for extraction. *R. alba maxima,* 'Jacobite Rose', 'Great Double White', double sport of the above, creamy flesh in centre on opening, showing a few stamens, few hips. 'Maiden's Blush', also known as 'Cuisse de Nymphe', 'La Royale', 'La Seduisante'; similar to *R. alba maxima,* but on opening the flowers have a warm flush of pink in the centre, fading paler.

Centifolia 'Rose of a Hundred Leaves', 'Cabbage Rose', 'Provence Rose'. Probably evolved during the seventeenth century from the above roses; to be seen in many Flemish pictures of the period (and hence called the 'Rose des Peintres'),

Moss', R. damascena bifera alba muscosa, 'Quatre Saisons Blanc Mousseux'. Like its parents it produces more than one crop of bloom.

Moss Apart from the above Damask Moss rose, *R. centifolia* gave rise in 1727 or earlier to a sport with 'mossy' buds, called *R. centifolia muscosa*, 'Common Moss'; similar to the parent but with less globular blooms, and with 'moss' all over the calyces and pedicel; the 'moss' is soft, sticky and fragrant.

Examples include 'Shailer's White' ('White Bath', 'Clifton Moss', *R. centifolia muscosa alba*); Shailer's sport was recorded in 1790, the others were probably identical to it. Similar to the pink form in every way except colour. 'Réné d'Anjou', recorded 1835, closely related to the 'Common Moss'; flowers opening rather flat, of lilac-pink, fully double, bronze young foliage. 'Single Moss', sports with fertile flowers occurred in England in 1807 and in France in 1814; they opened the way for seed raising and many hybrids occurred between the Damask Moss (which gave harsh 'moss' and a recurrent flowering habit), and the Centifolia Moss (which gave soft 'moss' and more handsome foliage and flowers).

Examples include 'Comtesse de Murinais' (recorded 1843), 'moss' green and harsh, flowers large, white, with pronounced 'button eye', not recurrent. 'Madame Delaroche-Lambert' (1873), rich purplish crimson, green 'moss' on long foliaceous sepals; recurrent. 'Salet' (1854), very similar to the 'Common

also on cretonnes and wallpapers up to the present day. Lax stems, thorny and prickly, making an open bush; large, rounded, coarsely toothed leaves, big, nodding, fully double flowers.

Examples include *R. centifolia* (of which the above description is typical). The variation *parvifolia (R. burgundica,* 'Pompon de Burgoyne', 'Pompon de St Francois'), believed to be a sport from the above, first recorded in 1664. Neat upright bushlet, tiny pointed leaves, tightly double rosette-flowers, deep pink. Probably arose as a witch's broom, a tightly bunched set of shoots stemming from the base (see Witch's Broom). There are two forms in cultivation, one stronger than the other. 'Unique Blanche' ('White Provence', 'Unique', 'Vierge de Cléry'), a sport from *R. centifolia,* recorded 1775; less vigorous than *R. centifolia,* otherwise similar but with less shapely white flowers opening from reddish buds. Variation *bullata* (lettuce-

leafed rose, 'Rose à feuilles de laitue'), a sport which originated in 1801. Distinguished by its large bullate leaves, brownish when young. Variation *cristata,* 'Crested Moss', 'Chapeau de Napoléon', a sport which originated in 1826, distinguished by the proliferous or crested calyx wings, so that the bud appears shrouded in greenery.

Autumn Damask R. gallica × *R. moschata. R. d. semperflorens (R. damascena bifera,* 'Quatre Saisons'), a small bush, with small thorns and prickles, downy leaves, bearing loose, double pink blooms at midsummer and again later, a character inherited from *R. moschata.* The 'Old Monthly' rose dates back to Roman and probably pre-Roman times. In 1835, it was reported that it had given rise to a sport bearing white flowers with pedicel and bud enclosed in bristly, 'mossy' excrescences; the 'moss' also appears on the surface of the leaves; this was named the 'Perpetual White Damask

Moss', but is markedly recurrent.

Further hybridisation The French empress, Napoleon Bonaparte's wife, Joséphine, collected in her garden at Malmaison, near Paris, all the roses she could acquire, and so started a fashionable interest in roses which has continued ever since. Her roses were recorded in the three series of paintings by Pierre Joseph Redouté (1759–1840). Copying the example of the Empress Joséphine seedlings were raised in ever-increasing quantities. Formerly distinct groups became hybridised and many of the most superb of the popular roses of the nineteenth century were difficult to ascribe to one group or another, except the Alba type which were less interbred.

Examples of highly bred Old Roses not distinctively attributable to any one group include 'Koenigin von Danemarck' (1816), showing considerable Alba influence in its greyish leaves, wide flat flowers, quartered and with 'button eyes', intense vermilion-pink in the centre on opening, fading paler. 'Madame Hardy' (1832), white, very full and cupped, faintly blush in the centre on opening, reflexing later and with green central pointel, Centifolia leaves. 'Cardinal de Richelieu' (1840), intense velvety maroon, cupped and reflexing, petals rolled at edges; smooth leaves.

Portland Roses At the end of the eighteenth century 'Slater's Crimson China' rose was introduced from Asia and in due course became hybridised with the Autumn Damask, the result being the 'Scarlet Four Seasons', 'Portland Rose' or *R. paestana*. Several more were subsequently raised, eventually giving rise to a group called Portland Roses, which bore at least two crops during the summer and autumn, some being in almost constant production.

Examples include 'Blanc de Vibert' (1847), yellowish green soft foliage, fully double, cupped blooms of white with a hint of lemon in the centre when opening. 'Comte de Chambord' (1860), pointed light green leaves, well filled flowers opening flat and reflexing, clear pink.

All of these roses distinctly derived from the Portland Rose inherit a very short pedicel; the leaves are gathered in a sort of collar quite closely under the flower. This is noticeable in 'Jacques Cartier' and also in some hybrid moss varieties, such as 'Gloire des Mousseux' and 'Mousseline'. The same character is also found in several hybrid perpetuals which are most closely linked to these roses, such as 'Baroness Rothschild' and 'Reine des Violettes'.

The style of flower most admired was one which was full of petals, expanding in a circle, flat or reflexing, apart from those mainly derived from *R. centifolia*, which were inclined to be globular or cup-shaped. Most appreciated was the fully open flower, not the bud. The colours range from white, blush white, maroon to purplish mauve and pink to bright crimson. 'Henri Martin' and 'Surpasse Tout' most nearly approached crimson, a colour which did not occur in roses except in those inheriting this true colour from 'Slater's Crimson China'. Flaked and striped varieties were much sought after and the subtly changing shades of the purplish varieties varied with the effect of light on them.

1 The deep-pink flowers of Rosa gallica 'Surpass Tout' are fully double.
2 Rosa gallica 'Cardinal Richelieu' has maroon flowers and reaches 4 feet.
3 Another old-fashioned Rose, Moss Rose, 'Henri Martin'.

Old shrub roses—a selection of 22, chosen for their floral perfection and garden value, including the historic main forms and hybrids

Name	Colour	Height
Belle de Crécy	Mauve	3 feet
Camaieux	Striped, mauve and white	3 feet
Capitaine John Ingram (Moss)	Maroon crimson	5 feet
Cardinal de Richelieu	Maroon	4 feet
Céleste	Clear pink	6 feet
Charles de Mills	Crimson purple	5 feet
Comte de Chambord	Pink	3 feet
Duc de Guiche	Crimson	5 feet
du Maître d'Ecole	Lilac	3 feet
Empress Josephine	Deep pink	3 feet
Fantin Latour	Blush pink	5 feet
Félicité Parmentier	Blush	4 feet
Général Kléber (Moss)	Bright pink	5 feet
Henri Martin (Moss)	Crimson	5 feet
Koenigin von Dänemarck	Pink	5 feet
Madame Hardy	White	6 feet
Maiden's Blush	Blush	6 feet
Président de Sèze	Mauve	5 feet
Réné d'Anjou (Moss)	Pink	4 feet
Surpasse Tout	Crimson	4 feet
Tour de Malakoff	Cerise and purple	7 feet
Tuscany Superb	Maroon	3 feet

1 Rose 'Constance Spry' is one of the recent introductions (1960) of the old-fashioned type of flower.
2 'Louise Odier', a Bourbon Rose.

Further Chinese hybrids The roses bred during the ancient Chinese civilisation reached Europe very early in the nineteenth century. They are believed to be hybrids between two species, *R. chinensis* and *R. gigantea,* and not only produced the rich crimson colouring found in 'Slater's Crimson China' but also pale yellow, as well as a habit of flowering from early summer until the onset of severe frost, coppery colouring. In popular esteem the pale yellow and coppery colours of the flowers outweighed the long flowering habit and made up for the small loose blooms, smooth small leaves, smooth weak stems with few prickles and general lack of vigour in all but the most suitably warm climates. While growers sought the recurrent habit by sowing seeds of these new types interpollinated with the established favourites, many varieties

were still being raised well into the 1850s which were untouched by either recurrent parent. At the same time the recurrent roses were eventually to come to the fore. There are the hybrids between the Autumn Damasks and 'Parson's Pink China', which we know today as the 'Old Blush' or 'Common China Rose'. In 1817, a seedling occurred between these two in the French island of Bourbon, and a subsequent seedling from this, raised in France about 1823, was called the Bourbon Rose. From this seedling many popular varieties were raised, which, while retaining much of the old style of flower, had smooth leaves; the most favoured were those which were recurrent.

Examples include 'Bourbon Queen' (1835), not recurrent, yet it is one of the roses most frequently found in old gardens; warm lilac pink, tall lax growth. 'Souvenir de la Malmaison' (1843), blush, very large, flat and full of petals, quartered, constantly in flower. The climbing sport, which has two good crops only, occurred in 1893 in Australia. 'Boule de Neige' (1867), white, double, camellia-like, an upright bush, constantly in flower. 'Reine Victoria' (1872), mallow pink, cupped, continuously in flower, spindly upright bush. The blush pink sport 'Madame Pierre Oger' has always been more popular.

Later developed varieties These include the semi-climbers 'Madame Isaac Pereire' (1880), large full flowers, quartered, of deep magenta pink, with two good crops, and the noted purple and white semi-climber 'Variegata di Bologna' (1909), which has fine, well-filled flowers but is not recurrent.

The selections from seed gradually produced tall bushes, bearing good rounded flowers in profusion at midsummer, with bunches of bloom later at the tips of the long new summer's growth. This led to them being called Hybrid Perpetual.

Non-recurrent varieties In addition to this ever-popular move towards perpetual roses many non-recurrent varieties continued to be raised, and several were tall lax bushes which today are used for covering stumps, hedgerows, etc. Good examples include *R. gallica violacea,* before 1802, semi-double, violet crimson, 6–7 feet. *R. dupontii,* before 1817, of *R. moschata* derivation, greyish leaves, single blush-white flowers, tall lax bush. *R. polliniana (R. macrantha* of gardens), before 1820, large single blush-pink, sprawling; 'Daisy Hill', 'Raubritter', 'Complicata' and 'Scintillation' are close relatives. 'Constance Spry', though introduced in 1960, being a hybrid between 'Belle Isis' (*R. gallica*) and 'Dainty Maid', assorts best with these roses. It makes a vigorous lax bush.

Other old hybrids Species other than those discussed above are normally classed under the related species Rosa, which contains many more varieties.

In 1583 *R. francofurtana* was described, said to be a hybrid between *R. gallica* and *R. cinnamosnea*. Two roses probably descended from this are *R. francofurtana* 'Agatha' and the much later rose known today as 'Empress Joséphine'. Once-flowering roses of *R. gallica* type, these are unique in having no thorns, ribbed leaves and large turbinate receptacles. 'Empress Joséphine' is worthy of inclusion in any collection of old roses.

Rambling and climbing roses All wild roses are shrubs but some are of lax habit and grow in somewhat shaded positions, reaching the sunlight by means of their hooked thorns which enable their stems to lodge in neighbouring bushes. All species of the *Synstylae* section of the genus, together with *R. chinensis*, *R. gigantea*, *R. laevigata*, *R. banksiae* and *R. bracteata* have these characters, and from these all climbing and rambling roses are derived. The last three species have produced little groups of related varieties but are not in the mainstream of breeding. The hybrids of *R. gigantea* and *R. chinensis*, evolved in China before their introduction into Europe between 1792 and 1824, were bushes not climbers, flowered from summer till autumn, and were comparatively large flowered. Practically all of the *Synstylae* species would be termed in horticulture 'ramblers', making long lax growths, bearing, with one exception, once only during the summer bunches of small single flowers. The exception is *R. moschata* whose flowers are borne from August onwards. British garden ramblers were derived from the *Synstylae* species *R. arvensis*, *R. sempervirens*, *R. multiflora*, *R. luciae* and *R. l.* var. *wichuraiana* (a few other species have played a small part) hybridised with other garden roses derived from the breeding together of *R. gallica* (see the section Old shrub roses), *R. moschata* and *R. phoenicea* on the one hand and the China hybrids mentioned above.

Rambling roses today include varieties raised from *R. arvensis* and *R. sempervirens* in the early nineteenth century, 'Félicité et Perpétué' and 'Adelaide d'Orleans'; from *R. multiflora*, 'Blush Rambler', 'Goldfinch'; from *R. luciae* var. *wichuraiana*, 'Dorothy Perkins', 'Excelsa', and *R. luciae*, 'Alberic Barbier', 'François Juranville', all in the early decades of this century. Very few have been raised since; one example is 'Crimson Shower'. Practically all rambling roses, apart from the hybrids of *R. luciae* itself (which had mainly tea roses for their other parent) are of white, pink, crimson or purplish colouring; those descended from *R. luciae* itself are mainly of yellowish or salmon colouring. Yellow also crops up in 'Aglaia' (*R. multiflora* × 'Rêve d'Or') which is the ancestor of the hybrid musk roses. Dwarf sports or hybrids of these roses gave rise to the polypoms or dwarf polyantha roses.

R. moschata crossed with the ancestral Chinese rose hybrids gave rise to the noisette class; the main selections, 'Blush Noisette', 'Aimée Vibert', bear small flowers in clusters repeatedly from summer till autumn. By hybridising more closely with the yellowish, ancestral Chinese roses the climbing teas were evolved, 'Gloire de Dijon', 'Maréchal Niel', in the middle decades of the eighteenth century. These may be regarded as among the first developments of what have come to be known in horticulture as 'climbing' roses, as opposed to 'rambling' roses; their distinguishing features are large flowers borne singly or in small clusters and a recurrent flowering habit. During the heyday of the hybrid tea roses numerous climbing sports occurred and are known as climbing HTs ('Climbing Madame Butterfly', 'Climbing Mrs Sam McGredy'); these reproduce the large flowers and leaf characters of the bush form and flower at least twice during the year. Their interest historically is mainly during the first half of this century. With the advent of the floribunda roses, towards the middle of this century, varieties have been bred with medium to large flowers borne singly and in clusters, flowering usually more repeatedly through the season than the climbing HTs ('Leverkusen', 'Soldier Boy'). With the fusion of the HTs and the 'floribundas' we may expect to see this group considerably increased in the future, augmented by sports from floribundas, and hybrids of 'Max Graf', which is descended from *R. rugosa* (*R. kordesii* and descendants).

1 Rambler Rose **'May Queen'**.
2 Climbing Rose **'Francis Lester'**.
3 **'Chaplin's Pink Companion'**, a climber.

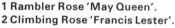

Rambling and climbing roses

Good ramblers mainly descended from *R. multiflora* and *R. luciae*, variety *wichuraiana*

Name	Colour
Crimson Shower	Crimson
Débutante	Pink
Excelsa	Scarlet crimson
Félicité et Perpetué	Milk white
Francis E. Lester	Blush, single
Goldfinch	Pale yellow
Sanders' White	White
Violette	Purple

Large-flowered ramblers mainly derived from *R. luciae*

Albéric Barbier	Creamy yellow
Albertine	Coppery pink
Breeze Hill	Straw yellow
Emily Gray	Yellow
François Juranville	Salmon pink
Mary Wallace	Pink
May Queen	Lilac pink
Paul Transon	Coppery pink

Climbers of hybrid tea style

Climbing Etoile de Hollande	Dark crimson
Climbing Mme Butterfly	Light pink
Climbing Mme Caroline Testout	Pink
Climbing McGredy's Ivory	White
Climbing Mrs Sam McGredy	Coppery Red
Easlea's Golden Rambler	Yellow
Guinée	Maroon
Mme Grégoire Staechelin	Deep pink
Paul's Lemon Pillar	Lemon white

Floribunda climbers

Climbing Allgold	Yellow
Coral Dawn	Coral pink
Danse du Feu	Orange red
Dream Girl	Coppery salmon
Kassel	Coppery red
Leverkusen	Pale yellow
Nymphenburg	Salmon pink
Parade	Crimson pink
Pink Cloud	Clear pink

1 'Albertine' and 'Zepherine Drouhin'.
2 'Emily Gray' (cream) and 'Danse du Feu'.

While some of the species of the *Synstylae* section may climb to 30 or 40 feet on trees (*R. filipes, R. brunonii*), the garden ramblers are usually not taller than 18 feet; the noisettes rather shorter; the climbing HTs up to 20 feet, and the floribunda-type moderns achieve 8–15 feet. These shorter roses, together with the tallest Bourbon roses and hybrid perpetual roses are frequently termed 'pillar' roses. A further variation is when rambling roses are budded on to stems of briar and develop umbrella-like heads; these are termed 'weeping standards'.

As the first crop of flowers of all of these classes is produced on shoots arising from the leaf-axils of the previous year's growth, the training of them on to pillars or poles, upright arches or vertically on walls will not tend to produce the maximum quantity of flower. By training the shoots nearly horizontally, flowering shoots will appear in every leaf axil. The modern pillar roses or floribunda climbers will benefit in the same way. Where they are growing vigorously, the pruning of

most rambling roses is by removing the wood of the previous season that has flowered immediately after flowering; if left for two seasons the flowering side-shoots may be shortened to one eye in winter. The hybrids of *R. luciae* do not require so much pruning as the hybrids of *R. multiflora* and *R. luciae*, var. *wichuraiana;* they are more bushy and flower freely from old twiggy branches. The same applies to 'Mermaid'. The recurrent flowering climbing roses should be pruned in winter, removing old twiggy growth and tying in long new shoots; and occasionally removing old wood as far as the base to encourage fresh growth.

R. banksiae and its forms and hybrids flower best on small side shoots; pruning consists in the occasional removal of old weak stems to encourage new, during the youth of the plant; thereafter little attention is required if the plants have sufficient space to develop on warm sunny walls.

The most natural way of enjoying rambling and climbing roses, particularly the more graceful varieties, is to

train them over hedgerows, stumps, arbours, and into trees. In ramblers the extreme grace of the falling sprays can then be appreciated, which is so much greater than when the sprays are trained upwards. An ideal method is to grow two roses in one tree, large and small flowered together to appreciate the contrast of style and form, and in such cultivation pruning is scarcely needed, nor possible. To any collection of rambling and climbing roses such old and unsurpassed favourites as 'Gloire de Dijon', 'New Dawn', 'Gruss an Teplitz', 'Mme Alfred Carrière', 'Climbing Monsieur Paul Lédé', 'Alister Stella Gray', 'Mermaid' and 'Climbing Lady Hillingdon' should be added, for their distinctive fragrance and strongly recurrent flowering habit. For warmer counties on sunny walls *R. banksiae* and its varieties are recommended, with small flowers early in the season, and 'Mermaid', a hybrid of *R. bracteata*.

12

A Gallery of Roses

*Apricot silk, a Hybrid Tea Rose of good fragrance
and fairly tall stature, bred from a seedling
of 'Souvenir de Jacques Verschuren'.*

Iceberg

(syn. Schneewittchen)

Colour: white
Type: Floribunda
Height: 2½–4 feet
Fragrance: strong
This very vigorous and branching rose has small, glossy, light green leaves, which are very resistant to disease. The buds flush shell-pink, but open to pure white double blooms, produced freely in large trusses. It is one of the best white Floribunda roses, and very popular. It has proved to be a first-rate bedding rose and is suitable for a 3-foot hedge.
Introduced: 1958
Breeder: Kordes, Germany
Parentage: 'Robin Hood' x 'Virgo'

Pascali

Colour: white
Type: Hybrid Tea
Height: 3–3½ feet
Fragrance: slight
A vigorous, upright grower, this has dark green, semi-glossy foliage. The flowers are double and are carried freely on tall upright growth, and may be cream or slightly shaded peach. Like most white roses it dislikes rain, but is probably the best white variety for cold areas. It is suitable for use in beds and borders.
Introduced: 1963
Breeder: Lens, Belgium
Parentage: 'Queen Elizabeth' x 'White Butterfly'

Schneezwerg

(syn. Snow Dwarf)

Colour: white
Type: R. *Rugosa* Shrub
Height: 4–5 feet
Fragrance: slight
A good bushy shrub with vigorous compact growth and small mid-green, glossy foliage, this bears rosette shaped, semi-double flowers, with regularly arranged petals around deep golden stamens. Although individual flowers do not last long, each bloom is perfectly shaped, and there is a constant succession from early summer to late autumn. Small orange-red hips appear in the autumn at the same time as the later blooms.
Introduced: 1912
Breeder: Lambert, Germany
Parentage: *R. rugosa* x white polyantha

Félicité et Perpétue

Colour: creamy-white
Type: R. *sempervirens* Rambler
Height: 12 feet or more
Fragrance: light, primrose-scented
An old, but still popular rose, this is a vigorous, graceful Rambler, suitable for growing over an arch or pergola, for training against a north wall, or planting to ramble in and over a hedge. The buds, flushed with crimson, open in summer to little creamy-white pompons, borne singly and in great clusters on the mass of twigs produced by the recommended light pruning. The shining dark leaves are almost evergreen.
Introduced: 1827
Breeder: Jacques, France
Parentage: *R. sempervirens*

Silver Moon

Colour: white
Type: Rambler
Height: to 40 feet
Fragrance: rich, apple-scented
This rambler is so vigorous that it may be allowed to climb at will into trees or over tall tree stumps, or trained over arches or pergolas. The medium-yellow buds open into large, semi-double white flowers with gold centres in midsummer. The leaves are a good glossy dark green. Prune only lightly.
Introduced: 1910
Breeder: Van Fleet, U.S.A.
Parentage: (*R. wichuraiana* x 'Devoniensis') x *R. laevigata*

Rosa Rugosa Alba

Colour: white
Type: Shrub (form of Species)
Height: 6 feet
Fragrance: strong, with a clove-like scent
This is the white form of the Ramanas or Japanese rose. It makes a vigorous bush and may be used to make a dense hedge, up to 6 feet thick, or grown as a specimen bush. It is an attractive rose, 'perpetual' flowering in that it produces its masses of 2½–3 inch wide flowers over a long period, well into the autumn when the bush is already crowded with orange-red hips from earlier flowers. The buds are tinted with pink. Plants may be left unpruned, or cut back fairly hard.
Introduced: after 1845
Parentage: form of *R. rugosa*

Iceberg

Pascali

Schneezwerg

Félicité et Perpétue

Silver Moon

Rosa rugosa alba

15

Rosa Primula

Colour: primrose-yellow
Type: Species
Height: 6 feet or taller
Fragrance: good, incense fragrance
Sometimes known as the 'Incense Rose' because of the aromatic fragrance of its leaves, this bears masses of small, primrose-yellow, single flowers in long sprays in early summer. Prune by removing in winter some of the oldest growths and small, twiggy shoots, after they have flowered. Left to itself, to develop as a shrub, it needs little pruning. The leaves are dark green, small and narrow.
Discovered about 1910

Rosa Cooperi

(syn. Cooper's Burmese Rose)

Colour: white
Type: Climber
Height: up to 25 feet
Fragrance: good, tea-scented
Not quite hardy enough for all gardens, this grows well in warm areas, especially if it is grown against a sheltered wall. The pure white blooms with wedge-shaped petals open around mid-summer. In the very mildest climates it may be grown as a Pillar rose or as an informal bush. The shining leaves give extra beauty. It needs only very light pruning.
Introduced: about 1931
Parentage: form of *R. gigantea*

Rosa x Alba Semi-Plena

(syn. R. Semi-Plena)

Colour: white
Type: Shrub—'Old' (medieval) rose
Height: 6 feet
Fragrance: moderate
This is one of the very old roses, cultivated in Europe for five or six centuries at least and supposed to be the 'White Rose of York' or a form of it. It is one of the roses grown in Bulgaria from which 'attar of roses' is distilled. The semi-double flowers, with a centre of gold stamens, smother the bush in mid-summer. The leaves are a dull, greyish-green. After the blooms come plentiful bright red hips.
Parentage: *Rosa* x *Alba (R. canina* x *R. damascena)*

Paul's Lemon Pillar

Colour: pale lemon, white at petal edges
Type: Climber (Hybrid Tea type)
Height: 15–20 feet
Fragrance: rich
Although this fine rose flowers once only, in summer, it is worth growing for the sake of its masses of large, well-shaped blooms. It is a vigorous plant, especially if it has a warm situation, away from searing winds. Otherwise, it makes an excellent Pillar rose, as its name implies.
Introduced: 1915
Breeder: Paul, England
Parentage: 'Frau Karl Druschki' x 'Maréchal Niel'

Frühlingsgold

(syn. Spring Gold)

Colour: creamy-yellow
Type: R. spinosissima Hybrid
Height: 6–7 feet
Fragrance: moderate
Flowering in early summer, this is one of the most graceful Shrub Roses. All along its arching stems it bears multitudes of soft yellow single blooms, 4–5 inches across, which fade to creamy-white, with golden centres. The delicious scent carries across the garden. Foliage is dense, and like all Spinosissima Hybrids, the branches are very prickly.
Introduced: 1937
Breeder: Kordes, Germany
Parentage: 'Joanna Hill' x *R. spinosissima hispida*

Maigold

Colour: bronze-yellow
Type: Modern Hybrid Shrub
Height: 7–10 feet
Fragrance: strong
Although usually classed as a Shrub Rose, this is regarded by some experts as a climber of moderate growth, reaching 10 feet against a wall or pillar in favourable situations. Grown as a shrub it is more likely to be 6–7 feet tall. The semi-double, cupped blooms, 4 inches across, grow freely in midsummer, with sporadic blooms after that. The flowers are set off by shining, dark green foliage. Dead-head regularly to ensure a longer succession of flowers.
Introduced: 1953
Breeder: Kordes, Germany
Parentage: 'Poulsen's Pink' x 'Frühlingstag'

Rosa Primula

Rosa 'Cooperi'

Rosa x Alba Semi-Plena

Paul's Lemon Pillar

Frühlingsgold

Maigold

17

Golden Melody

(syn. Irene Churruca)

Colour: yellow
Type: Hybrid Tea
Height: 2½ feet
Fragrance: rich
This is a yellow rose, opening to a buff colour and fading to cream. The blooms are well shaped on long stems, making it a favourite for cutting for flower arrangement. The growth is vigorous and spreading, but the bronze-tinted foliage can be rather coarse. The blooms stand up to wet weather better than most of this colour.
Introduced: 1934
Breeder: La Florida, Spain
Parentage: 'Madame Butterfly' x 'Lady Hillingdon' x 'Souvenir de Claudius Pernet'

Elegance

Colour: yellow
Type: Climber (Hybrid Tea type)
Height: 10–15 feet
Fragrance: slight
A vigorous Climber with dark glossy foliage, this will produce large full-petalled, clear yellow blooms, deeper gold at the centre, which fade nearly to white. It is free-flowering in the early summer but does not produce many blooms later in the season. It will quickly cover a fence or may be trained over an arch.
Introduced: 1937
Breeder: Brownell, U.S.A.
Parentage: 'Glenn Dale' x 'Mary Wallace' seedling

Mermaid

Colour: primrose-yellow
Type: Climber
Height: up to 30 feet
Fragrance: slight
This excellent Climber is very often a slow starter, but it will produce large blooms continuously from midsummer through to winter. The pale primrose-yellow blooms with a mass of amber stamens open into flat single flowers, 5–6 inches across, and the dark glossy dark green foliage is almost evergreen. The young stems are very brittle, so take care when training to give some support. Once established, it will grow vigorously, and will not require pruning.
Introduced: 1917
Breeder: Paul, England
Parentage: *R. bracteata* x yellow Tea Rose

Grandpa Dickson

(syn. Irish Gold)

Colour: lemon-yellow
Type: Hybrid Tea
Height: 3–3½ feet
Fragrance: slight
The full petalled blooms are deep lemon-yellow, and fade to cream with pink edges as they age. They are perfectly shaped and are carried on tall, upright growth, with dark green glossy foliage. Flowers come early and will continue through into the autumn. The blooms last well, both on the plant and as cut flowers.
Introduced: 1966
Breeder: Dickson & Sons, N. Ireland
Parentage: ('Perfecta' x 'Govenador Braga da Crus') x 'Piccadilly'

Courvoisier

Colour: ochre-yellow
Type: Floribunda (Hybrid Tea type)
Height: 2½–3½ feet
Fragrance: strong
Upright in growth, this makes an excellent bush for bedding purposes. The large, Hybrid Tea type flowers, up to 4 inches across, are carried either singly or several to a cluster. They are fully double and well shaped, with a strong, pleasing fragrance. The leaves are a shining, medium green.
Introduced: 1966
Breeder: McGredy, N. Ireland
Parentage: 'Elizabeth of Glamis' x 'Casanova'

Peer Gynt

Colour: yellow
Type: Hybrid Tea
Height: 3 feet
Fragrance: slight
This makes a vigorous branching plant, with ample dark green leathery foliage. Throughout the summer and autumn it flowers almost continuously. The rich canary yellow fully double blooms tend to turn to light peach as they age, particularly in hot weather. The petal edges are slightly fringed.
Introduced: 1968
Breeder: Kordes, Germany
Parentage: 'Colour Wonder' x 'Golden Giant'

Golden Melody

Elegance

Mermaid

Grandpa Dickson

Courvoisier

Peer Gynt

Helen Traubel

Colour: apricot-pink
Type: Hybrid Tea
Height: 3½ feet
Fragrance: sweet
This is a lovely rose with long pointed buds opening into large, high-centred blooms measuring 5–6 inches across, which become flat as they age. Sometimes the outer petals have wavy edges. It is very free-flowering and exceptionally good in the autumn. The dull green foliage is plentiful and although rather tall, the vigorous growth is upright.
Introduced: 1951
Breeder: Swim (Armstrong Nurseries), U.S.A.
Parentage: 'Charlotte Armstrong' x 'Glowing Sunset'

Casanova

Colour: yellow
Type: Hybrid Tea
Height: 4½ feet
Fragrance: fairly strong
This is one of the taller Hybrid Tea varieties, developing into an upright bush, vigorous in habit, with dark green glossy leaves with a leathery texture. The flowers are large, up to five inches in diameter when fully open. The yellow gradually changes to a pleasant buff as the blooms age, and it is probably at its best in autumn.
Introduced: 1964
Breeder: McGredy, N. Ireland
Parentage: 'Queen Elizabeth' x 'Perfecta'

Goldbusch

Colour: golden-yellow
Type: Modern Hybrid Shrub
Height: 4–8 feet
Fragrance: good, raspberry scented
The coral-pink buds open to shapely, semi-double, golden-yellow flowers, with golden stamens. The main flush of blooms is in midsummer, but flowers go on afterwards. The plant will make a spreading bush, perhaps 6 feet through in time, or may be trained as a Pillar rose. To encourage the maximum number of flowers cut away any weak growth in late winter, reduce long, wandering shoots by a third and cut back side growths to three buds.
Introduced: 1954
Breeder: Kordes, Germany
Parentage: 'Golden Glow' x *R. rubiginosa* hybrid

Peace

Colour: yellow
Type: Hybrid Tea
Height: 4–5 feet
Fragrance: moderate
This rose has won the medal for the best bloom at the Royal National Rose Society Shows more times than any other variety. It is very vigorous with glossy leathery foliage. The blooms are large, about 6 inches across, perfectly shaped, and are clear lemon yellow with rosy edges. Prune very lightly, and leave it to grow into a large free-flowering shrub.
Introduced: 1942
Breeder: Meilland, France
Parentage: ('George Dickson' x 'Souvenir de Claudius Pernet') x ('Joanna Hill' x 'Charles P. Kilham') x 'Margaret McGredy'

Elizabeth Harkness

Colour: cream
Type: Hybrid Tea
Height: 3 feet
Fragrance: sweet
This is an early blooming variety which will go on flowering all through the summer. The large full blooms usually appear singly and are a cream-buff colour, tinged with pink at the petal edges. The growth is upright and bushy with mid-green foliage. The blooms are useful for exhibition.
Introduced: 1969
Breeder: Harkness, England
Parentage: 'Red Dandy' x 'Piccadilly'

Gruss an Aachen

Colour: creamy flesh-pink, deeper in the centre
Type: Floribunda (see below)
Height: 3–4 feet
Fragrance: good
Although listed in modern catalogues as a Floribunda rose, this was earlier classified as a Dwarf Hybrid Polyantha. It grows vigorously flowers freely and is suitable for bedding purposes. The large double flowers open flat and are creamy flesh-pink with deeper pink in the folds. It needs only moderate pruning.
Introduced: 1909
Breeder: Geduldig, Germany
Parentage: 'Frau Karl Druschki' x 'Franz Deegen'

Helen Traubel

Casanova

Goldbusch

Peace

Elizabeth Harkness

Gruss an Aachen

Golden Showers

Colour: golden-yellow
Type: Climber
Height: 6–10 feet
Fragrance: moderate
This very free-flowering rose is most suitable
for fences and trellises, and will make an
excellent pillar rose or hedge or may be grown
as a large shrub. The long, pointed, golden buds,
produced both singly and in clusters, open into
large semi-double flattish blooms measuring 3–4
inches across. The flowers are produced
continuously throughout the summer. The dark
green, bronze tinted glossy foliage contrasts
well with the blooms.
Introduced: 1956
Breeder, Lammerts, U.S.A.
Parentage: 'Charlotte Armstrong' x 'Capt.
Thomas'

Goldgleam

Colour: brilliant canary-yellow
Type: Floribunda
Height: 2½–3½ feet
Fragrance: some
One of the finest of all light yellow
Floribundas, this flowers very freely right
through the summer and autumn. Although of
medium height only, it is a vigorous, branching
plant, with glossy leaves, bronze as they unfold
in spring. The colour is weather-resistant and
unfading.
Introduced: 1966
Breeder: Le Grice, England
Parentage: 'Gleaming' x 'Allgold'

Allgold

Colour: bright yellow
Type: Floribunda
Height: 2½ feet
Fragrance: moderate
Probably the best deep yellow Floribunda yet
produced, this is an exceptionally fine bedding
rose. The clear buttercup-yellow blooms grow in
small clusters of semi-double flowers, and
retain the colour all through the summer,
showing no sign of fading. The bush starts to
flower very early and will continue until the
frost. Growth is bushy and vigorous and the
dark glossy foliage is plentiful.
Introduced: 1956
Breeder: Le Grice, England
Parentage: 'Goldilocks' x 'Ellinor Le Grice'

Canary Bird

(*R. xanthina spontanea*)

Colour: canary-yellow
Type: form of Species (*R. xanthina*)
Height: to 6 feet
Fragrance: nil
Of all the spring-flowering roses, this has the
largest and brightest flowers, which accounts
for its popularity. The single blooms, 2½
inches in diameter, usually flower most freely
in late spring on long arching stems, which have
bright green, fern-like leaves. It is best grown
as a specimen, when it will make a bush 5
to 6 feet thick and equally tall. Prune to
remove winter-killed wood, dying stems and
the oldest shoots, to encourage new ones.
Introduced: 1907
Parentage: thought to be *R. xanthina*

Circus

Colour: bicolor
Type: Floribunda
Height: 2 feet
Fragrance: strong
The dwarf habit makes this a useful rose for the
front of the border. It makes a dazzling
display as the flowers are first yellow, then
change to pink and red as they age. The blooms
are produced in both small and large clusters,
and the plant has plenty of dark green foliage.
The bushes are vigorous, compact and sturdy.
Introduced: 1956
Breeder: Swim (Armstrong Nurseries), U.S.A.
Parentage: 'Fandango' x 'Pinocchio'

Sutter's Gold

Colour: golden-yellow
Type: Hybrid Tea
Height: 4 feet
Fragrance: strong
This is a good distinctive rose with few thorns
and lovely greenish-bronze foliage. The buds
are shaded crimson and pink, but open into
deep golden double flowers 4–5 inches across.
The blooms are borne on long stems, which
makes this a good rose for cutting. It branches
freely, is a fine bedding rose and the blooms are
resistant to rain.
Introduced: 1949
Breeder: Swim (Armstrong Nurseries), U.S.A.
Parentage: 'Charlotte Armstrong' x 'Signora'

Golden Showers

Goldgleam

Allgold

Canary Bird

Circus

Sutter's Gold

Whisky Mac

Colour: golden orange
Type: Hybrid Tea
Height: 2½–3 feet
One of the newer roses in this unusual colour range, this has medium sized blooms, but they are very shapely and full. It makes a fairly low bush and so is ideal for bedding purposes. The opening leaves are bronze, changing to a shining dark green.
Introduced: 1968
Breeder: Tantau, Germany
Parentage: not recorded

Meg

Colour: apricot
Type: Climber
Height: 8 feet
Fragrance: slight
This moderately vigorous rose makes an extremely good Pillar rose, and will give a beautiful display of large, flat, semi-double, apricot-yellow blooms all through the summer. The clusters contrast well with the dark glossy foliage. It can also be grown on a wall or fence, when it may reach 15 to 20 feet.
Introduced: 1954
Breeder: Gosset, England
Parentage: probably 'Paul's Lemon Pillar' x 'Mme. Butterfly'

Southampton

Colour: orange
Type: Floribunda
Height: 3–3½ feet
Fragrance: slight
This is one of the newest additions to the Floribundas in this colour range. The blooms are fairly full of petals, which may be better described as apricot-orange, slightly flushed with scarlet on the reverse. The foliage is a good, shining bright green and the plant is vigorous and free flowering.
Introduced: 1972
Breeder: Harkness, England
Parentage: ('Ann Elizabeth' x 'Allgold') x 'Yellow Cushion'

Shepherd's Delight

Colour: orange
Type: Floribunda
Height: 3 feet
Fragrance: slight
Red sky at night means Shepherd's Delight, and this rose is aptly named. The brilliant display of flame, orange and yellow blooms, semi-double and of medium size, are produced in clusters, and continue to flower all through the summer, the colour becoming paler in the autumn. The growth is very vigorous with matt, dark green foliage, which stands up well to all weathers. It will make an excellent shrub.
Introduced: 1958
Breeder: Dickson, N. Ireland
Parentage: 'Masquerade' seedling x 'Joanna Hill'

Manx Queen

(syn. Isle of Man)

Colour: gold
Type: Floribunda
Height: 3 feet
Fragrance: moderate
This rose is a rich golden colour flushed with bronze and red towards the outer edges of the petals. The blooms, of moderate size, are produced in large open clusters with plentiful dark green foliage, and the growth is compact and bushy, making it an excellent variety for bedding.
Introduced: 1963
Breeder: Dickson, N. Ireland
Parentage: 'Shepherd's Delight' x 'Circus'

Rosa Foetida Bicolor

Colour: orange-copper, yellow on reverse of petals
Type: Sport or form of Species
Height: 4–5 feet
Fragrance: heavy
The Capucine Rose was grown in Britain before 1590. Although it is worth growing as a specimen Shrub, it is, perhaps, more noteworthy as entering into the parentage of many of the modern orange and flame-coloured Hybrid Tea varieties. It produces its single blooms very freely in early summer. Prune lightly: cut away the oldest stems in winter and, after flowering is over, prune off those twiggy growths that have produced flowers.
Introduced: before 1590
Parentage: Sport or form of *R. foetida*

Whisky Mac

Meg

Southampton

Shepherd's Delight

Manx Queen

Rosa Foetida Bicolor

25

Typhoon

Colour: bronze-pink
Type: Hybrid Tea
Height: 3 feet
Fragrance: strong
This is a vigorous plant with glossy, medium-green leaves. Its flowers are large, well-formed and full-petalled with a tinge of yellow to their bronze-pink. This rose begins to flower in early summer and repeats blooming freely. Experience since its recent introduction indicates that its growth is clean, healthy and not prone to disease.
Introduced: 1972
Breeder: Kordes, Germany
Parentage: 'Colour Wonder' x 'Doctor Verhage'

Alexander

Colour: vermilion
Type: Hybrid Tea
Height: 4 feet
Fragrance: very slight
This newly-introduced rose, which is named in honour of Field Marshal Earl Alexander of Tunis, is an upright, strong growing tree with dark, shiny green leaves. Its brilliant vermilion flowers are large but, being moderately full (20 petals), they have been found to be able to stand up well to bad weather. It appears to be very hardy and makes a good plant for a rose hedge.
Introduced: 1972
Breeder: Harkness, England
Parentage: 'Super Star' x ('Ann Elizabeth' x 'Allgold')

Joseph's Coat

Colour: golden-yellow
Type: Semi-Climber or tall Shrub
Height: 6–8 feet
Fragrance: slight
This is best described as a vigorous, tall Shrub, rather than a semi-climber. It can be grown as an isolated, specimen bush, but is probably best treated as a Pillar rose. The golden flowers, edged with red and veined with orange, are double, fairly full, and are borne in clusters. The main flush of flowers is in summer, but there is a good crop in autumn, particularly after deadheading. Prune by removing the oldest shoots.
Introduced: 1964
Breeder: Armstrong, U.S.A.
Parentage: 'Buccaneer' x 'Circus'

Esther Ofarim

Colour: bicolor
Type: Floribunda (Hybrid Tea type)
Height: 2 feet
Fragrance: very slight
This rose is a dwarf, bushy and compact. Its leaves are medium-green, and matt in texture. It has full orange-red and yellow blooms (about 30 petals), which are borne several together on a stem and in trusses. It makes a long-lasting cut flower and is an excellent rose for growing under glass.
Introduced: 1971
Breeder: Kordes, Germany
Parentage: 'Colour Wonder' x 'Zorina'

Princess Michiko

Colour: orange
Type: Floribunda
Height: 3–3½ feet
Fragrance: slight
This has been described as 'the brightest and most startling of all orange Floribundas' and those who like this colour will probably agree. The well-shaped semi-double blooms, which fade to a reddish-orange as they become older, have a touch of gold at the bases of their petals. They are produced in large clusters. It makes a vigorous plant, of upright habit, its foliage dark green, tinted with copper.
Introduced: 1966
Breeder: Dickson, N. Ireland
Parentage: 'Spartan' x 'Circus'

Coventry Cathedral

Colour: light vermilion
Type: Floribunda (Hybrid Tea type)
Height: 3 feet
Fragrance: very slight
This free-flowering rose is an upright and branching bush. It has medium-green, semi-glossy leaves. Its profuse flowers are moderately full. The petals are light vermilion on their inner surfaces, but their outer sides are a paler shade. They are produced several together on a stem and in trusses. The plant appears to be healthy and vigorous and its foliage is resistant to disease.
Introduced: 1972
Breeder: McGredy, N. Ireland
Parentage: ('Little Darling' x 'Goldilocks') x 'Irish Mist'

Typhoon

Alexander

Joseph's Coat

Esther Ofarim

Princess Michiko

Coventry Cathedral

New Dawn

(syn. Everblooming Dr W. Van Fleet)

Colour: blush-pink
Type: Climber (Hybrid Tea type)
Height: 15–20 feet (wall); 8 feet (pillar)
Fragrance: sweet

Although not as vigorous as 'Dr W. Van Fleet', this has been a popular rose for over 40 years, because of its sweetly fragrant, silvery-pink, well-shaped blooms, very freely borne in clusters. It flowers early, around midsummer, carries on flowering for many weeks and blooms again in the autumn. It reaches its maximum height when trained against a wall.
Introduced: 1930
Discovered by: Dreer, U.S.A.
Parentage: Sport of 'Dr W. Van Fleet'

Rosa Macrantha

Colour: blush-pink
Type: Hybrid between two Species
Height: 4–5 feet
Fragrance: sweet

This is best grown as a lax bush in less formal parts of the garden or in front of other shrubs. It bears large, sweetly fragrant, single blooms in midsummer. They pale almost to white as they age and are followed by large, round red hips. The Hybrid has produced several named varieties when crossed with other roses, some with semi-double flowers. Do not prune hard; merely cut away some of the oldest growths after flowering is over.
Introduced: 1823
Parentage: *R. gallica* x *R. canina*

Madame Pierre Oger

Colour: creamy blush-pink
Type: Bourbon Shrub
Height: 5–6 feet
Fragrance: strong

One of the best-known and popular of all the old Shrub roses, this makes an erect slender bush. It flowers very freely, the first flush in midsummer followed by blooms produced intermittently until autumn. Although the cup-shaped flowers are described as creamy blush-pink, the colour varies with the weather, from almost white to deep rose. The Shrub shows to its best advantage when grown as an isolated specimen.
Introduced: 1878
Discovered by: Oger, France
Parentage: Sport of 'La Reine Victoria'

Michèle Meilland

Colour: salmon-pink
Type: Hybrid Tea
Height: 2½–3 feet
Fragrance: slight

The soft delicate colour of this rose and the fact that it is good for cutting, makes it useful for the flower arranger. It is very widely grown in New Zealand, especially the climbing form. The high-centred, well-shaped blooms, moderate in size, are produced freely on long stems with bright green foliage. Growth is vigorous. A good bedding rose which grows well in town gardens.
Introduced: 1945
Breeder: Meilland, France
Parentage: 'Joanna Hill' x 'Peace'

Kathleen Harrop

Colour: shell-pink
Type: Bourbon Climber
Height: 5–6 feet
Fragrance: sweet

Although classed as a Bourbon Climber, this fine rose is more suitable as a Pillar rose, or for making a hedge or screen. A Sport from the ever-popular 'Zéphirine Drouhin', it is thornless like its parent. The pretty semi-double pink flowers, crimson on the back of the petals, are borne in clusters throughout the summer and autumn. Prune in late winter, cutting back the longest shoots by a third and removing any very old twiggy wood entirely.
Introduced: 1919
Discovered by: Dickson, N. Ireland
Parentage: Sport of 'Zéphirine Drouhin'

Fritz Nobis

Colour: pink
Type: Modern Hybrid Shrub
Height: 4–6 feet
Fragrance: good, clove-scented

One of the most free-flowering of Shrub roses, this makes a much-branched, bushy plant, as wide across as it is high. The sweetly-scented semi-double flowers, flesh-pink, slightly flushed with salmon, appear about midsummer and for a few weeks thereafter. They are followed by reddish hips. The foliage is a good glossy green. Prune in late winter by cutting away the oldest growths.
Introduced: 1940
Breeder: Kordes, Germany
Parentage: 'Joanna Hill' x *R. rubiginosa magnifica*

New Dawn

Rosa Macrantha

Madame Pierre Oger

Michèle Meilland

Kathleen Harrop

Fritz Nobis

Rosa Micrugosa

Colour: blush-pink
Type: Hybrid between two Species
Height: 6 feet
Fragrance: slight
Where there is room for it, bearing in mind that it may make a fairly dense shrub 6 feet tall and as much across, this rose is worth a place in the garden. It bears large, single flowers, up to 5 inches across in midsummer. The blooms, pale blush-pink in colour, have the added attraction of a central boss of creamy stamens. They are followed by round, bristly orange-red hips.
Introduced: Before 1905
Parentage: *R. roxburghii* x *R. rugosa*

Lavender Lassie

Colour: lilac-pink
Type: Shrub
Height: 3½–5 feet
Fragrance: very sweet, musk fragrance
This rose can be grown as a specimen bush or will make a good ornamental hedge continuously covered in rosette shaped lilac-pink flowers which open flat. The blooms, measuring three inches across, are borne in trusses. The plant is of bushy, vigorous habit and is very tall. If it is not over-pruned, it may grow to 6 feet.
Introduced: 1959
Breeder: Kordes, Germany
Parentage: not recorded

Blue Moon

(syns. Mainzner Fastnacht, Sissi)

Colour: silvery lilac-blue
Type: Hybrid Tea
Height: 2½–3½ feet
Fragrance: strong lemon fragrance
Roses of this colour are becoming increasingly popular since the introduction of 'Sterling Silver' (one of the parents of this rose) in 1957. 'Blue Moon' makes a vigorous bush, upright in habit, with reddish-brown stems and glossy, mid-green leaves. The buds are pointed, the blooms well shaped and full. Flower arrangers like its colour and long stems.
Introduced: 1964
Breeder: Tantau, Germany
Parentage: an unnamed seedling x 'Sterling Silver'

Albertine

Colour: coppery-pink
Type: Rambler
Height: 12-18 feet
Fragrance: strong
After all these years, this is still one of the best of Ramblers, although it is a difficult rose to handle because it is so thorny. The loosely double flowers are borne very freely along the stiff stems; a single, mature plant may produce hundreds of blooms from early summer onwards, to fill the garden with fragrance. It may either be pruned fairly hard or left unpruned except for the removal of the oldest stems.
Introduced: 1921
Breeder: Barbier, France
Parentage: *R. wichuraiana* x 'Mrs A. R. Waddell'

Rosa Mundi

(syn. *R. gallica versicolor*)

Colour: crimson, striped and splashed with pink and white
Type: Gallica Shrub
Height: 3-4 feet
Fragrance: little or none
This gaily-coloured Shrub rose is always associated with collections of old garden roses, but is often mistakenly called the 'York and Lancaster Rose' (which is *R. damascena versicolor*). It flowers very freely during the midsummer. Excellent as a specimen bush, it also makes a fine low hedge as it needs little pruning other than the occasional cutting away of the very oldest shoots after flowering.
Introduced: before 1500
Parentage: Sport from *R. gallica officinalis*

Blue Diamond

Colour: lavender-mauve
Type: Floribunda (Hybrid Tea type)
Height: 2½-3 feet
Fragrance: good
The large flowers, typical of the Floribunda Hybrid Tea type, are borne in large clusters. They begin to appear early in the season and go on throughout summer and autumn. Both the leaves and the stems are purplish-bronze in colour. It makes a vigorous, compact bush and the unusual colour of its flowers makes it a popular variety with flower arrangers.
Introduced: 1963
Breeder: Lens, Belgium
Parentage: 'Purpurine' x ('Purpurine' x 'Royal Tan')

Rosa Micrugosa

Lavender Lassie

Blue Moon

Albertine

Rosa Mundi

Blue Diamond

Madame Caroline Testout

Colour: bright rose-pink with darker centre and soft carmine edges
Type: Hybrid Tea
Height: 3–3½ feet
Fragrance: slight
At over 80 years of age, this must be considered as one of the older Hybrid Tea varieties still in cultivation. It remains a vigorous, well-liked rose, even though its full-petalled blooms sometimes 'ball' (fail to open properly) in damp, overcast weather. In 1902 it produced a Climbing Sport, a popular rose for training against a wall, because of its large flowers.
Introduced: 1890
Breeder: Pernet-Ducher, France
Parentage: 'Mme de Tartas' x 'Lady Mary Fitzwilliam'

Madame Butterfly

Colour: pale pink
Type: Hybrid Tea
Height: 3–3½ feet
Fragrance: strong and sweet
This is an old variety, but probably still the best of its type. The well-formed medium-sized blooms are pink with shadings of gold and apricot and are borne on long stems with few thorns. It flowers freely and is good for cutting and growing under glass. The growth is vigorous and bushy. There is a climbing Sport of this variety (Smith 1925) which is useful for pillars and arches, as well as for walls facing south or west.
Introduced: 1918
Discovered by: Hill, U.S.A.
Parentage: Sport of 'Ophelia'

Constance Spry

Colour: rose-pink
Type: Modern Shrub Rose
Height: 5-6 feet or more
Fragrance: rich, myrrh-scented
This fine rose is named for the famous flower arranger, who did so much to popularize the art. The blooms, produced around midsummer and for some weeks afterwards, are large and fully double, cup-shaped and richly fragrant. They are produced very freely along the branches. When they first appear the leaves are tinged with red, eventually becoming dark green.
Introduced: 1961
Breeder: Austin, England
Parentage: 'Belle Isis' x Dainty Maid'

Monique

Colour: pink
Type: Hybrid Tea
Height: 4 feet
Fragrance: strong
The well-shaped, large full blooms are produced on long stems, which makes this a good rose for cutting. The flowers are a silvery-pink, shaded with salmon-pink at the base. The plant is very vigorous, upright and branching. It produces flowers freely, and the rich green pointed foliage is plentiful.
Introduced: 1949
Breeder: Paolino, France
Parentage: 'Lady Sylvia' x unnamed seedling

Aloha

Colour: pink
Type: Large-Flowered Climber
Height: 8–10 feet
Fragrance: moderate
This is a particularly good Pillar rose and will readily reach 8 to 10 feet, or it may be grown as a large bush. It is perpetual-flowering and will continue through the summer and do particularly well in the autumn. The blooms, on long stems, are large, double and well-formed, coloured rose-pink with a deeper shade on the reverse. The dark and leathery foliage contrasts well.
Introduced: 1955
Breeder: Boerner, U.S.A.
Parentage: 'Mercedes Gallart' x 'New Dawn'

August Seebauer

Colour: rich rose-pink
Type: Floribunda (Hybrid Tea type)
Height: 4-5 feet
Fragrance: slight
The large blooms, up to 3 inches in diameter, fully double, are carried in large clusters throughout the season. The plant is vigorous in growth, among the taller of the Floribundas with Hybrid Tea-type blooms, and flowers freely. The leaves are a good glossy green. It is a lovely rose, which might have been more popular under a different name.
Introduced: 1944
Breeder: Kordes, Germany
Parentage: 'Break o'Day' x 'Else Poulsen'

Madame Caroline Testout

Madame Butterfly

Constance Spry

Monique

Aloha

August Seebauer

Jeanne de Montfort

Colour: rich pink
Type: Moss
Height: 6-8 feet
Fragrance: sweet
This is a very vigorous Moss Rose which, if left to itself, with little pruning, may make a bush 6 feet across, so allow it ample room to display its large clusters of warm pink flowers. These appear mainly in midsummer, with a few later blooms. The flowers are enhanced by the yellow stamens. The stems and buds are thickly covered with sticky, fragrant 'moss' (glandular appendages), characteristic of the group.
Introduced: 1851
Breeder: Robert, France
Parentage: derived from *R. centifolia*

Ma Perkins

Colour: pink
Type: Floribunda
Height: 2 feet
Fragrance: sweet
The flowers are double and cup-shaped and are borne in small trusses. They are shell-pink, flushed with apricot, paling towards the edge of the petals. The foliage is a rich glossy green and the growth is vigorous and bushy. It is an excellent bedding rose.
Introduced: 1952
Breeder: Boerner, Jackson & Perkins, U.S.A.
Parentage: 'Red Radiance' x 'Fashion'

Pink Elizabeth Arden

(syn. Geisha)

Colour: soft pink
Type: Floribunda
Height: 3 feet
Fragrance: slight
This rose is bushy and compact in growth. It has semi-glossy, medium green leaves. Its blooms are moderately full (with about 35 petals) and quite large, being 2½-3 inches in diameter, and are produced in large clusters. It has been found to be a hardy rose since its fairly recent introduction.
Introduced: 1964
Breeder: Tantau, Germany
Parentage: Not disclosed

Pink Parfait

Colour: pink
Type: Floribunda (Hybrid Tea type)
Height: 2–4 feet
Fragrance: slight to moderate
This is an upright, compact, vigorous rose, ideal for bedding, and which stands up well to wet weather. The Hybrid Tea type blooms are a blend of pinks, deepening towards the edges of petals, yellow at the base and apricot on the reverse. The colour will not fade in the sun, and it is likely to intensify during cooler weather. It is free-flowering with medium green foliage and is very good for cutting.
Introduced: 1962
Breeder: Swim, U.S.A.
Parentage: 'First Love' x 'Pinocchio'

Dearest

Colour: pink
Type: Floribunda
Height: 2½ feet
Fragrance: sweet
The authentic description of this colouring is pale geranium lake—and it has been described as one of the best pinks in its class. The free-flowering blooms are displayed in well-spaced trusses and open into large flat flowers. It is particularly noted for its fragrance, as this is not a common feature in Floribundas. The strong stems and dark glossy foliage, together with a vigorous and bushy habit, make this a perfect bedding rose, though it dislikes wet weather.
Introduced: 1960
Breeder: Dickson, N. Ireland
Parentage: Seedling from 'Spartan'

Prima Ballerina

(syn. Première Ballerine)

Colour: cherry-pink
Type: Hybrid Tea
Height: 3 feet
Fragrance: very strong
The fragrance of this rose alone makes it worth a place in any garden and it is a popular decorative flower. The cherry-pink, semi-double blooms are 4 inches across, and a good shape with high pointed centres. The stiff stems have plentiful light green foliage, and the growth is vigorous and upright. This is a reliable rose even during a wet summer.
Introduced: 1958
Breeder: Tantau, Germany
Parentage: unknown seedling x 'Peace'

Jeanne de Montfort

Ma Perkins

Pink Elizabeth Arden

Pink Parfait

Dearest

Prima Ballerina

Yesterday

Colour: pink, with silvery base deepening to purple at the edges of petals
Type: Floribunda
Height: 3 feet
Fragrance: good
This rose has a vigorous, bushy and spreading habit. Its semi-glossy leaves are small and light green. It has a unique flowering habit of blooming very continuously. Its flowers are semi-double, flat, 1 inch in diameter, and have 13 small petals. The stamens are pronounced. The blooms are borne in trusses.
Introduced: To be introduced in autumn 1974
Breeder: Harkness, England
Parentage: ('Phyllis Bide' x 'Shepherd's Delight') x 'Ballerina'

Queen Elizabeth

Colour: light pink
Type: Floribunda (Hybrid Tea type)
Height: 6 feet
Fragrance: slight
The well-shaped Hybrid Tea-type blooms are a clear light pink borne on long, almost thornless stems, and make excellent cut flowers. They are produced both singly and in clusters of 3-9, and flower profusely in summer and autumn. It is a healthy, vigorous rose, with abundant, glossy, mid-green foliage, and left to itself will grow to 6 feet or more, but careful pruning will keep the height down to 4-5 feet. Although tall for bedding it will make an excellent hedge if bushes are planted 1½-2 feet apart.
Introduced: 1955
Breeder: Lammerts, U.S.A.
Parentage: 'Charlotte Armstrong' x 'Floradora'

Shannon

Colour: bright deep pink
Type: Hybrid Tea
Height: 4 feet or more
Fragrance: none
This makes a tall, upright plant with full flowers, excellent for exhibition purposes, for cutting for the house or for garden display. As the blooms are so full, they may tend to 'ball' in wet weather, but in warm, bright conditions this is one of the best of this colour range. The foliage is a good, glossy green.
Introduced: 1965
Breeder: McGredy, N. Ireland
Parentage: 'Queen Elizabeth' x 'McGredy's Yellow'

Rosa Rugosa Scabrosa

Colour: magenta
Type: form of Species
Height: 4 feet
Fragrance: strong, clove-scented
This is one of the Ramanas or Japanese roses. It has very large single flowers, up to 5 inches in diameter when fully open, the colour sometimes described as fuchsia pink, sometimes soft magenta. The main flush is in midsummer, but is followed by many other blooms. The hips are very large and can reach 1½ inches in diameter. The leaves turn bright yellow in autumn before they fall. The plant will make an interesting hedge of medium height.
Introduced: probably later half of 19th century
Parentage: form of *R. rugosa*

Sarah van Fleet

Colour: rose-pink
Type: *R. rugosa* Hybrid
Height: 5-6 feet
Fragrance: rich, clove-scented
Another of the roses derived from the species *R. rugosa*, the Ramanas or Japanese rose, this makes a fine shrub, or may be used to form a rose hedge. It flowers very freely, particularly in midsummer, producing its large semi-double blooms in clusters. The cream-coloured stamens add to the attraction of the flowers. The newly-developing foliage is bronze, later changing to a bright, glossy green.
Introduced: 1926
Breeder: Van Fleet, U.S.A.
Parentage: *R. rugosa* x 'My Maryland'

Lady Seton

Colour: rosy-pink, flushed salmon
Type: Hybrid Tea
Height: 4 feet or more
Fragrance: rich
Lady Seton, after whom this fine rose is named, is better known as Julia Clements, the flower arranger who has done so much to popularize the art. Fittingly, the blooms are produced on long stems, making them useful for cutting. The plant makes a tall, upright shrub and the flowers are produced continuously throughout the season: particularly good crops appear in autumn. The foliage is a good mid-green.
Introduced: 1966
Breeder: McGredy, N. Ireland
Parentage: 'Ma Perkins' x 'Mischief'

Yesterday

Shannon

Rosa Rugosa Scabrosa

Sarah van Fleet

Lady Seton

Handel

Colour: cream, edged deep pink
Type: Climber
Height: 10-15 feet
Fragrance: slight
The breeder of this rose describes it as 'A most unusual Climber with cream flowers edged deep rose-pink. One of my most successful roses.' Anyone who has seen it in full flower in summer is hardly likely to disagree. The flowers are large, flowering throughout the season, and the foliage is dark green slightly tinged with bronze. It makes a good specimen for training against a wall, or as a Pillar rose.
Introduced: 1965
Breeder: McGredy, N. Ireland
Parentage: 'Heidelberg' x 'Columbine'

Stella

Colour: cream, flushed pink
Type: Hybrid Tea
Height: 2½–3 feet
Fragrance: sweet
This is a rose for the exhibitor. The blooms, produced on stiff stems, are large and measure up to five inches across. They are cream, flushed pink with the colour deepening to carmine at the edges of the petals, and are high-centred and well-formed. The growth is vigorous and upright with an abundance of dark green foliage which will stand up well to wet weather.
Introduced: 1959
Breeder: Tantau, Germany
Parentage: 'Horstmann's Jubiläumsrose' x 'Peace'

Kerryman

Colour: pink
Type: Floribunda (Hybrid Tea type)
Height: 2½ feet
Fragrance: very slight
This is a bushy and compact rose with semi-glossy, grained, medium-green leaves. It blooms profusely during the season. The blooms are full and almost the size of Hybrid Tea roses. The outer petals are a deeper pink, and the colour intensifies as the blooms age. They are borne several together on one stem. This variety has been found to be reasonably hardy since its recent introduction.
Introduced: 1970
Breeder: McGredy, N. Ireland
Parentage: 'Paddy McGredy' x ('Mme. Leon Cuny' x 'Columbine')

Erfurt

Colour: pink
Type: Modern Shrub
Height: 4-5 feet
Fragrance: strong and musky
Although the colour of this delightful Shrub rose is officially described as carmine, much of the centre of each semi-double bloom is citron-yellow, with a central boss of yellow stamens. It is almost continuously in bloom from early summer until the end of the season. The newly developing foliage is a good bronze. The bush will eventually make a specimen as wide as it is high.
Introduced: 1939
Breeder: Kordes, Germany
Parentage: 'Eva' x 'Réveil Dijonnais'

Daily Sketch

Colour: pink bicolor
Type: Floribunda (Hybrid Tea type)
Height: 2½-3 feet
Fragrance: strong
This is an attractive free-flowering deep pink and silver bicolor Floribunda with Hybrid Tea type blooms. Because the full flowers are borne on strong stems in well-spaced clusters they are ideal for use in indoor arrangements. The perfectly shaped blooms may measure up to 3½ inches across. In contrast with many varieties, the pink becomes deeper, instead of paler, as the blooms age. The vigorous growth makes this variety suitable for bedding.
Introduced: 1960
Breeder: McGredy, N. Ireland
Parentage: 'Ma Perkins' x 'Grand Gala'

Picasso

Colour: carmine with deeper blotches, silvery reverse
Type: Floribunda
Height: 2 feet
Fragrance: slight
This is a rose that colourwise defies description. Its breeder calls it a 'hand-painted' rose. It grows bushy and compact, with small, matt, medium-green leaves. Its flowers are moderately full, having 25 petals. They are carried severally on one stem and in large trusses. 'Picasso' is an unusual rose that attracts flower-arrangers.
Introduced: 1971
Breeder: McGredy, N. Ireland
Parentage: 'Marlene' x ['Evelyn Fison' x ('Orange Sweetheart' x 'Frühlingsmorgen')]

Handel

Stella

Kerryman

Erfurt

Daily Sketch

Picasso

39

Michèlle

Colour: salmon pink
Type: Floribunda
Height: 2½-3 feet
Fragrance: very strong
This variety is upright and vigorous in growth.
Its leaves are matt and light green in colour.
It has moderately full flowers, which are 3
inches in diameter and have 25 petals. They are
produced very freely and continuously
throughout the summer. So far it has been
found to be healthy. It is an excellent button-
hole rose.
Introduced: 1970
Breeder: De Ruiter, Holland
Parentage: Seedling x 'Orange Sensation'

Spartan

Colour: rich salmon to light red
Type: Floribunda (Hybrid Tea type)
Height: 2½ feet
Fragrance: slight
Being the earliest Floribunda/Hybrid Tea type
rose, this variety is of interest historically.
It is a vigorous, upright grower, with small
semi-glossy, medium green, leaves which are
tinted bronze. It is very free-flowering with
large, very full salmon-coloured flowers, which
are 3½ inches in diameter. Unfortunately it
does not like rain, which causes its blooms to
'ball', and it has a tendency to disease.
Introduced: 1954
Breeder: Boerner, Jackson and Perkins, U.S.A.
Parentage: 'Geranium Red' x 'Fashion'

Gipsy Moth

Colour: salmon
Type: Floribunda (Hybrid Tea type)
Height: 2½ feet
Fragrance: moderate
This rose is vigorous and branching in its
growth, and is an ideal bedding rose. Its
full, salmon-coloured blooms, which have 30
petals, are perfect Hybrid Tea in form, and are
carried several together on stiff, upright stems.
Introduced: 1969
Breeder: Tantau, Germany
Parentage: Not disclosed

Kathleen Ferrier

Colour: salmon-pink
Type: Floribunda
Height: 4 feet or more
Fragrance: light
This rose commemorates the famous English
singer. The semi-double flowers, individually
about 2½ inches across when fully open, are
carried in small clusters on long stems. The
plant flowers freely throughout the season,
especially if it is regularly dead-headed. The
leaves are dark, shining green. Like other tall
Floribundas, it makes a good hedging rose, but
for this purpose should be lightly pruned only.
Introduced: 1955
Breeder: Buisman, Holland
Parentage: 'Gartenstolz' x 'Shot Silk'

Westminster

Colour: red and yellow
Type: Hybrid Tea
Height: 3-3½ feet
Fragrance: strong
To describe the colour of this rose as red
and yellow is really inadequate. The petals are
red on their insides and yellow on their
reverses, with red stripes and splashes. The
blooms are large, full of petals and very fragrant.
The young leaves are tinged with bronze, later
becoming glossy green. The plant makes an
upright, somewhat open bush.
Introduced: 1959
Breeder: Robinson, England
Parentage: 'Gay Crusader' x 'Peace'

Gail Borden

Colour: bicolor
Type: Hybrid Tea
Height: 2½ feet
Fragrance: slight
This is a fine, colourful bedding rose, and one
that is good for exhibition. It is very
vigorous and upright with dark leathery foliage.
Although not abundant, the pale orange-yellow
buds, carried on strong stems, open into deep
pink flowers, creamy-yellow on the reverse.
They are excellent for cutting.
Introduced: 1956
Breeder: Kordes, Germany
Parentage: 'Mev. H.A. Verschuren' x 'Viktoria
Adelheid'

Michèlle

Spartan

Gipsy Moth

Kathleen Ferrier

Westminster

Gail Borden

Elizabeth of Glamis

(syn. Irish Beauty)

Colour: salmon
Type: Floribunda
Height: 3 feet
Fragrance: rich and strong
The strong fragrance of this rose has been described as 'cinnamon-scented' and makes this a Floribunda to be remembered. The salmon blooms are shaded peach and open into flat double flowers measuring 3-4 inches across. It is free flowering with large, well-spaced trusses and produces a constant display of colour throughout the summer. It is vigorous and makes a shapely bush with mid-green foliage.
Introduced: 1964
Breeder: McGredy, N. Ireland
Parentage: 'Spartan' x 'Highlight'

My Choice

Colour: pale carmine, reverse buff
Type: Hybrid Tea
Height: 3-4 feet
Fragrance: rich
The yellow-suffused carmine buds open into large well-formed blooms of carmine with buff or cream reverse, high centred and measuring 4-5 inches across. The early-flowering blooms are produced freely on upright stems and when cut will last well in water. They are also suitable for exhibition. Weather resistance is good and the strong growth is tall and bushy with dark green foliage.
Introduced: 1958
Breeder: Le Grice, England
Parentage: 'Wellworth' x 'Ena Harkness'

Glengarry

Colour: bright vermilion
Type: Floribunda (Hybrid Tea type)
Height: 2½-3 feet
Fragrance: slight
This colour has become increasingly popular in recent years, though it is not easy to match with other colours. The best way of displaying roses of this colour in the rose garden is by planting them in separate beds, where the colours of their blooms do not clash with others. The large flowers, up to 4 inches in diameter, are borne either singly or in small clusters, on compact bushy plants with semi-glossy leaves.
Introduced: 1969
Breeder: Cocker, Scotland
Parentage: 'Evelyn Fison' x 'Wendy Cussons'

Fred Loads

Colour: vermilion
Type: Floribunda Shrub
Height: 4½-5 feet
Fragrance: slight
This is a vigorous, tall, upright-growing plant which can grow to 5 feet or more, and is particularly suitable for a rose hedge, at the back of a rose bed or in shrub border. It can also be used as a specimen. It flowers continuously through the summer and autumn, producing an abundance of large heads of single, orange-vermilion blooms. The healthy foliage is plentiful, and is a glossy light green.
Introduced: 1967
Breeder: Holmes, England
Parentage: 'Orange Sensation' x 'Dorothy Wheatcroft'

Kalahari

Colour: salmon-pink
Type: Hybrid Tea
Height: 2½ feet
Fragrance: slight
This is a vigorous rose that produces very profuse dark green foliage. Its salmon-coloured flowers are full (about 35 petals), large and very freely produced. It is a rose that stands up to bad weather very well.
Introduced: 1971
Breeder: McGredy, N. Ireland
Parentage: ('Hamburger Phoenix' x 'Danse du Feu') x 'Uncle Walter'

Orangeade

Colour: bright orange
Type: Floribunda
Height: 2 feet
Fragrance: slight, but sweet
This weather-resistant Floribunda often starts to flower singly, but later freely produces trusses of brilliant orange semi-double blooms which turn to reddish orange as they age. The bronze-green foliage is round and plentiful and the growth vigorous, branching and bushy. It is an excellent variety to grow in a small garden.
Introduced: 1959
Breeder: McGredy, N. Ireland
Parentage: 'Orange Sweetheart' x 'Independence'

Elizabeth of Glamis

My Choice

Glengarry

Fred Loads

Kalahari

Orangeade

43

Climbing Shot Silk

Colour: orange-salmon
Type: Climbing Hybrid Tea
Height: 12 feet
Fragrance: very strong
One of the best of its type, this very vigorous Climber is a sport from the attractive Hybrid Tea variety. It produces in small clusters a good supply of beautiful deep salmon-pink blooms with yellow bases, and is particularly suitable for walls, fences and pergolas. The leaves are glossy mid-green.
Introduced: 1937
Breeder: Prince, England
Parentage: 'Hugh Dickson' seedling x 'Sunstar'

Anna Wheatcroft

Colour: light vermilion
Type: Floribunda
Height: 2½ feet
Fragrance: slight
This rose is an exceptional colour, light orange-vermilion, and the elegant buds open into flat single or semi-double flowers measuring 3½-4 inches across, displaying golden stamens. The clusters of about 5 blooms are well-spaced and very free-flowering and, if cut in the bud stage, will last well in water. The growth is vigorous and bushy with abundant dark green, semi-glossy foliage. It is a variety which resists wet weather well.
Introduced: 1959
Breeder: Tantau, Germany
Parentage: 'Cinnabar' x unknown seedling

Anne Cocker

Colour: vermilion
Type: Floribunda
Height: 3 feet
Fragrance: slight
This rose is a strong, upright grower with an abundance of semi-glossy, dark green foliage. It flowers very freely with trusses of medium-sized, full, light vermilion blooms. The flowers begin to bloom a little late in the season but continue well until frosts begin. It has excellent keeping properties when cut which makes it very attractive to floral arrangers.
Introduced: 1971
Breeder: Cocker, Scotland
Parentage: 'Highlight' x 'Colour Wonder'

Stroller

Colour: bicolor
Type: Floribunda
Height: 2½ feet
Fragrance: very slight
Named after the successful British show-jumping horse, this is a rose of vigorous, bushy growth with foliage that is glossy and dark green. Its gold and cerise flowers are moderately full (24 petals) and grow either singly on a stem or in trusses. It repeat-flowers quickly. It is a hardy plant and is claimed by its breeder to be disease-resistant.
Introduced: 1968
Breeder: Dickson, N. Ireland
Parentage: 'Manx Queen' x 'Happy Event'

Réveil Dijonnais

Colour: bicolor
Type: Modern Shrub rose or Climber
Height: 6-8 feet
Fragrance: good
This shrub blooms almost continuously from early summer to late autumn. The flowers, which are semi-double with 14 petals, have bright yellow centres. They are about 4 inches in diameter and are borne in small clusters. The leaves are a good glossy green. It is of moderate vigour only, so may be grown as a tall Shrub, or trained against a wall or pillar.
Introduced: 1931
Breeder: Bautois, France
Parentage: 'Eugene Fürst' x 'Constance'

Masquerade

Colour: bicolor
Type: Floribunda
Height: 3 feet or more
Fragrance: slight
This is very effective when grown as a hedge or as an isolated shrub. The small yellow buds open into yellow flowers then turn to pink deepening to dark red, making a marvellous display when all the colours appear on one truss at the same time. Although individual flowers are small, the trusses are large. The very vigorous strong growth produces a tall plant if it is lightly pruned. The foliage is dark green and leathery.
Introduced: 1950
Breeder: Boerner, Jackson & Perkins, U.S.A.
Parentage: 'Goldilocks' x 'Holiday'

Climbing Shot Silk

Anna Wheatcroft

Anne Cocker

Stroller

Réveil Dijonnais

Masquerade

Adair Roche

Colour: pink with silver reverse
Type: Floribunda (Hybrid Tea type)
Height: 3 feet
Fragrance: slight
This rose is a vigorous, upright grower. It has glossy, medium-green foliage. It flowers freely producing full, large blooms, which have 30 petals and are 5 inches in diameter, borne in generous trusses. The flowers are so like Hybrid Teas in size and shape that the breeder classifies this variety, contrary to the official designation, as a 'Hybrid Tea rose'.
Introduced: 1969
Breeder: McGredy, N. Ireland
Parentage: 'Paddy McGredy' x 'Femina' seedling

Sarah Arnot

Colour: pink
Type: Hybrid Tea
Height: 2-2½ feet
Fragrance: sweet
The colour of this variety is a warm rose-pink, and the evenly displayed blooms are well formed with high centres. The sweetly-perfumed flowers are produced freely, and may measure up to 4½ inches in diameter. They resist wet weather well. The leathery, mid-green foliage is very abundant, and similar to that of one of its parents, 'Peace'. The growth is vigorous and upright, though the plant is not very tall.
Introduced: 1956
Breeder: Croll, Scotland
Parentage: 'Ena Harkness' x 'Peace'

Chicago Peace

Colour: blend of pink, yellow and copper
Type: Hybrid Tea
Height: 4-5 feet
Fragrance: slight
A Sport from the famous 'Peace', this has equally large flowers, up to 6 inches in diameter, very full of petals. Like its parent it is a vigorous variety, which makes a tall bush. The leaves are dark, shining green.
Introduced: 1962
Breeder: Johnston, U.S.A.
Parentage: Sport from 'Peace'

Ballet

Colour: pink
Type: Hybrid Tea
Height: 2½ feet
Fragrance: very slight
This is a great favourite with the rose exhibitor. The perfectly-formed blooms, carried on strong stems, measure about 5 inches across and the curled petals reveal a high pointed centre which retains its shape well. It is a deep pink and, with its attractive matt grey-green foliage, is also popular with flower arrangers. The growth is vigorous and upright, but not tall, which makes it a useful plant for bedding purposes.
Introduced: 1958
Breeder: Kordes, Germany
Parentage: 'Florex' x 'Karl Herbst'

Norwich Pink

Colour: carmine-pink
Type: Climber
Height: 8-12 feet
Fragrance: little or none
This is another of the modern Climbers bred by Herr Wilhelm Kordes known as *Kordesii* Climbers. It is a 'perpetual' flowering kind, in that it produces its blooms throughout the season. The carmine-pink, semi-double flowers, officially described as bright cerise, are very showy and their attractiveness is enhanced by the yellow stamens. It is excellent as a Pillar rose or may be trained against a wall or fence.
Introduced: 1962
Breeder: Kordes, Germany
Parentage: not disclosed

Rose of Tralee

Colour: deep pink
Type: Floribunda
Height: 3 feet
The large, deep pink double blooms are shaded salmon and are produced in clusters. Individual flowers measure up to 4 inches across. They are borne in profusion throughout the summer. The vigorous bushy growth bears small, matt dark green foliage.
Introduced: 1964
Breeder: McGredy, N. Ireland
Parentage: 'Leverkusen' x 'Korona'

Adair Roche

Sarah Arnot

Chicago Peace

Ballet

Norwich Pink

Rose of Tralee

Roseraie de l'Hay

Colour: crimson-purple
Type: Rugosa Shrub
Height: 6-7 feet
Fragrance: strong, clove-scented
One of the loveliest of the 'Ramanas' or Japanese roses (derived from *R. rugosa*), this always excites admiration when seen in collections of older roses, simply because of the colour of its blooms. They are produced continuously from early summer onwards and are very large, though somewhat loose in form. Little pruning is needed, although cutting back the shoots once they have flowered will help to prolong the flowering season.
Introduced: 1901
Breeder: Cochet-Cochet, France
Parentage: *R. rugosa* Hybrid

Sunday Times

Colour: rosy pink
Type: Floribunda
Height: 1½-2 feet
Fragrance: slight
This rose grows into a dwarf, bushy and compact bush, which is particularly thorny. It makes very excellent ground cover with its profusion of small, dark green, semi-glossy foliage and rose-pink blooms. Its flowers are full with 28 petals and are borne singly on individual stems and in trusses.
Introduced: 1971
Breeder: McGredy, N. Ireland
Parentage: ('Little Darling' x 'Goldilocks') x 'München'

Norman Hartnell

Colour: deep cerise to light crimson
Type: Hybrid Tea
Height: 3½-4 feet
Fragrance: slight to medium
Named after the famous dress-designer, this rose has well-formed buds which open to fairly full, large blooms, 5-5½ inches across when fully developed. They retain their colour well, even in wet weather. They are excellent for exhibition purposes as well as for garden decoration. The plants are tall, bushy in growth, with ample foliage which is tinged with copper when the leaves first develop.
Introduced: 1964
Breeder: Kordes, Germany

Zéphirine Drouhin

Colour: carmine-pink
Type: Bourbon Climber
Height: 10 feet
Fragrance: strong
This is a very vigorous perpetual-flowering rose for use as a hedge, training on pillars or on south or west-facing walls. The flat, semi-double, medium-sized blooms, borne on thornless stems, are a bright carmine-pink and are plentiful during the summer and autumn. The soft light green foliage is tinted red. Although this rose is a climber, it can also be pegged down to form a shrub. It is necessary to keep a constant watch for mildew, but the plant is well worth a place in the garden.
Introduced: 1868
Breeder: Bizot, France

Moussu de Japon

(syn. 'Japonica')

Colour: mauve
Type: Old Shrub Rose (Moss)
Height: 2 feet
The shoots, buds, leaf-stalks and even the surfaces of the leaves of this variety are covered with dense, emerald-green moss. The shrub grows slowly, making a dense thicket. Around midsummer and for some weeks afterwards, it bears multitudes of smallish flowers, which are magenta-rose when they first open, but fade quickly to greyish-lilac. The young leaves are attractive, flushed with lilac and copper tones.
Introduced: 19th century
Parentage: derived from *R. centifolia*

Ramona

Colour: crimson-cerise
Type: Rambler
Height: 12-15 feet
Fragrance: good
The single blooms, up to 4 inches across, grey on the reverses of the petals, begin to appear in early summer and for many weeks thereafter, until early autumn. The leaves are a good shiny green, with three leaflets only. Although it is hardy in all but the very coldest places, it is best trained against a wall.
Introduced: 1913
Parentage: Sport from *R. anemonoides*

Roseraie de l'Hay

Sunday Times

Norman Hartnell

Zéphirine Drouhin

Moussu de Japon

Ramona

Will Scarlet

Colour: scarlet-crimson
Type: Shrub (Hybrid Musk)
Height: 5-6 feet
Fragrance: slight
This rose is well named. The buds are a bright scarlet, and open into semi-double scarlet-crimson flowers, paling towards the centre, which are borne very freely in medium-sized clusters throughout the season. It will make a spectacular Shrub with a fine display of blooms, followed by orange hips. It is a Sport from 'Wilhelm', but the growth is not so vigorous as that of the parent, although the blooms are a little more fragrant.
Introduced: 1952
Breeder: Hilling, England
Parentage: Sport from 'Wilhelm'

News

Colour: purple
Type: Floribunda
Height: 3 feet
This is a new colour break for the Floribunda group. The buds are wine-red, opening to a rich, clear purple which, instead of fading with age, becomes more intense. The colour is highlighted by the central cluster of bright golden anthers. The plant is vigorous and produces its flowers freely throughout the season.
Introduced: 1969
Breeder: Le Grice, England
Parentage: 'Lilac Charm' x 'Tuscany Superb'

Zigeuner Knabe

(syn. Gypsy Boy)

Colour: crimson-purple
Type: Shrub (Bourbon Hybrid)
Height: 5 feet
Fragrance: slight
This is a well-known Shrub rose, which usually excites admiration when it is seen among a collection of older roses. It makes a vigorous bush, as much deep as it is high, bearing, from midsummer onwards for several weeks, hundreds of flat, crimson-purple blooms, the petals touched with white at the base. Little pruning is needed, except for the removal of very twiggy shoots in late winter.
Introduced: 1909
Breeder: Lambert, Germany

William Lobb

(syns. Duchesse d'Istrie, Old Velvet Moss)

Colour: purple
Type: Moss Shrub
Height: 6 feet
Fragrance: moderate
The beautiful colour of this variety varies from dark crimson-purple, to mauve and pale lilac grey, and when fully open the semi-double blooms are large with muddled centres. The colour makes it a favourite rose with flower arrangers. There is plenty of 'moss' on the buds, borne in clusters on strong shoots. This can be rather an ungainly Shrub, and it is a good idea to plant a group for an illusion of depth.
Introduced: 1855
Breeder: Laffay, France
Parentage: derived from *R. centifolia*

Beatrice

Colour: deep rose-pink
Type: Floribunda
Height: 3 feet
Fragrance: slight
This rose grows to an upright bush. It has abundant medium-green foliage. It is very free-flowering. Its blooms are very full with 50 petals. They are loosely formed, are about 4½ inches in diameter and are carried in trusses. Its flowers last well.
Introduced: 1968
Breeder: McGredy, N. Ireland
Parentage: 'Paddy McGredy' x ('Perfecta' x 'Montezuma')

Wendy Cussons

Colour: cerise
Type: Hybrid Tea
Height: 2½-3 feet
Fragrance: strong
This is an outstanding rose, the colour of which has been described as sparkling cerise and its scent is one that is associated with the older roses. The full, shapely blooms open to 5 inches across and flower all through the summer and into autumn. The plant is vigorous, upright and branching with glossy, dark green foliage, and does not mind wet weather.
Introduced: 1959
Breeder: Gregory, England
Parentage: 'Independence' x 'Eden Rose'

Will Scarlet

News

Zigeuner Knabe

William Lobb

Beatrice

Wendy Cussons

Céleste

(syn. Celestial)

Colour: clear soft pink
Type: Old Shrub Rose (Alba)
Height: 5-6 feet
Fragrance: light
One of the most charming of the Old Garden Roses this makes a strong, upright growing bush, well furnished with soft greyish-green foliage. The well-shaped, semi-double clear pink blooms, which are enhanced by a ring of golden stamens, contrast well with the leaves. The plant flowers around midsummer and for some weeks afterwards. Little pruning is needed, except for the removal of dead or dying wood, and the bush does not sprawl or make untidy growths.
Introduced: late 18th century
Parentage: derived from *R. alba*

Louise Odier

Colour: rich soft pink
Type: Old Shrub Rose (Bourbon)
Height: 5-6 feet
Fragrance: sweet
This makes a vigorous bush, compact in habit and thus ideal for a lawn specimen, especially as its delightful, perfectly shaped flowers are produced over a long period. After the first early summer flush is over, blooms will continue to appear until late autumn. The rounded double blooms have their petals so regularly arranged that they are reminiscent of a camellia and their soft pink is faintly flushed with lilac. Little pruning is needed.
Introduced: 1851
Breeder: Margottin, France
Parentage: unknown, but complex

Charm of Paris

(syn. Parisier Charme)

Colour: pink
Type: Floribunda (Hybrid Tea type)
Height: 2½ feet
Fragrance: sweet
This rose is a close relation of 'Fragrant Cloud' and has many of its characteristics. The double blooms, borne in clusters, are large, full and well formed, and a beautiful shade of silvery pink. The strong sweet perfume is an added attraction. The growth is vigorous and branching, with an abundance of healthy, glossy, dark green foliage. It is ideal as a bedding rose, and is at its best in dry weather.
Introduced: 1965
Breeder: Tantau, Germany
Parentage: 'Prima Ballerina' x 'Montezuma'

Pink Grootendorst

Colour: pink
Type: Rugosa Shrub
Height: 4 feet
Fragrance: none
This is a Sport from 'F. J. Grootendorst', and many rose-fanciers consider it to be superior to its parent. The small blooms, borne in clusters, are rose-pink, with the edges of the petals fringed, like those of a garden pink. It is very free and continuous-flowering and a favourite for indoor arrangements. The foliage is mid-green and is produced on very prickly stems. The plant makes a reasonably compact shrub, as much across as it is high.
Introduced: 1923
Breeder: Grootendorst, Holland
Parentage: Sport from 'F. J. Grootendorst'

Lady Sylvia

Colour: light pink
Type: Hybrid Tea
Height: 3 feet
Fragrance: strong
This is an excellent rose for the flower arranger. It will last well in water, and has a clear fresh scent. The medium-sized shapely blooms are a rosy salmon-pink shaded apricot at the base, and borne on long stems with few thorns. The growth is vigorous with plentiful small mid-green foliage. It is useful for growing under glass, in pots or in beds.
Introduced: 1927
Breeder: Stevens, England
Parentage: Sport of 'Madame Butterfly'

Parade

Colour: carmine-crimson
Type: Climber
Height: 8-10 feet or more
Fragrance: good
This is one of the best of the newer climbing roses, although it was introduced nearly twenty years ago. The full blooms are borne fairly continuously but mainly in two flushes—in summer and early autumn. The flowers are large and are carried in clusters; the plant is vigorous, branching well. When they first open the leaves are flushed with coppery-red, later turning a good glossy green. The plant may be trained against a wall, fence or pillar.
Introduced: 1957
Breeder: Boerner, Jackson & Perkins, U.S.A.
Parentage: 'New Dawn' seedling x 'World's Fair'

Céleste

Louise Odier

Charm of Paris

Pink Grootendorst

Lady Sylvia

Parade

J. S. Armstrong

Colour: crimson
Type: Hybrid Tea
Height: 3-3½ feet
Fragrance: slight
This was an All-America Rose Selection in 1962, the year after it was introduced, and it is certainly a fine addition to this desirable colour range. The medium-sized flowers, up to 4½ inches across when open, are freely borne in clusters throughout the season, with good crops in autumn. The colour holds well even in bad weather. Growth is vigorous and the leaves, bronze-tinged at first, become a good dark green.
Introduced: 1961
Breeder: Swim, U.S.A.
Parentage: 'Charlotte Armstrong' x unnamed seedling

Super Star

(syn. Tropicana)

Colour: vermilion
Type: Hybrid Tea
Height: 4 feet
Fragrance: sweet
This has well formed, medium-sized blooms, the vermilion colour quite brilliant, without shading. The blooms are produced very freely, as is the dark green foliage. It is vigorous, and grows tall for a Hybrid Tea type. The blooms are good for cutting, and the plant grows well under glass.
Introduced: 1960
Breeder: Tantau, Germany
Parentage: Parentage unregistered (but thought to be a seedling x 'Peace' x a seedling x 'Alpine Glow')

Highlight

Colour: orange-scarlet
Type: Floribunda
Height: 2½ feet
Fragrance: slight
This rose is aptly named and will high-light any garden, even on a dull day. The brilliant orange-scarlet, free-flowering, semi-double blooms are well-shaped and borne in large well-spaced clusters. In order to preserve the brightness it is advisable to remove any individual flowers which fade in the sun. The large, dark green foliage is produced in abundance on plants which are vigorous, upright, bushy and healthy.
Introduced: 1958
Breeder: Robinson, England
Parentage: Seedling x 'Independence'

Poulsen's Supreme

Colour: pink
Type: Floribunda
Height: 2½ feet
Fragrance: slight
This rose has sturdy, erect growth with abundant light green foliage. Its flowers are semi-double, with 8-20 petals. The free-flowering pink blooms are about 3 inches in diameter and are borne in trusses.
Introduced: 1945
Breeder: Poulsen, Denmark
Parentage: 'Poulsen's Pink' x a seedling

Lilli Marlene

Colour: crimson
Type: Floribunda
Height: 2½ feet
Fragrance: slight
This is an excellent bedding rose, and still one of the best of the Floribundas. The large, semi-double blooms are borne in moderately-sized, well-spaced trusses and are a rich velvety crimson. When opened they reveal attractive bright yellow stamens. It is a vigorous bush with abundant leathery foliage which is prone to mildew. Altogether it can be used to great effect.
Introduced: 1959
Breeder: Kordes, Germany
Parentage: 'Our Princess' x 'Rudolph Timm'

Curiosity

Colour: red with yellow reverse
Type: Hybrid Tea
Height: 2 feet
Fragrance: slight
This low-growing variety has unusual foliage, unlike that of any other known rose. When young its leaves are reddish, variegated with cream; as they mature the red changes to green, but the cream becomes more pronounced. The blooms are not exceptional. It is for its unique, extremely decorative foliage that 'Curiosity' is primarily sought after by flower arrangers and garden planners.
Introduced: 1971
Breeder: Cocker, Scotland
Parentage: 'Cleopatra' Sport

J. S. Armstrong

Super Star

Highlight

Poulsen's Supreme

Lilli Marlene

Curiosity

Alec's Red

Colour: cherry red
Type: Hybrid Tea
Height: 3 feet
Fragrance: rich and sweet
A criticism applied to modern roses in general is that they have little or no fragrance. It certainly does not apply to this variety which is so sweetly scented that it was awarded the Harry Edland Memorial Medal for fragrance in 1969, the year before it was introduced to the rose-growing public. The well-formed flowers are carried on strong, upright stems which bear ample glossy green foliage.
Introduced: 1970
Breeder: Cocker, Scotland
Parentage: 'Fragrant Cloud' x 'Dame de Coeur'

Ena Harkness

Colour: crimson-scarlet
Type: Hybrid Tea
Height: 2½ feet
Fragrance: sweet
This is undoubtedly one of the best red varieties. It flowers freely and produces large, full, high-centred blooms. However, in some situations the blooms may tend to droop, but this can be overcome by feeding the plant, and keeping the soil moist in dry weather. It is vigorous and upright with leathery, medium green leaves.
There is a Climbing Sport (Murrell 1954), also a vigorous grower, which produces good blooms.
Introduced: 1946
Breeder: Norman, England
Parentage: 'Southport' x 'Crimson Glory'

Stephen Langdon

Colour: deep scarlet
Type: Floribunda (Hybrid Tea type)
Height: 2½ feet
Fragrance: slight
This is a beautiful rose with matt, deep green leaves and upright growth. Its deep scarlet Hybrid Tea-type flowers are produced freely, both singly on a stem or in trusses, later in the season than average. The blooms are moderately full and have about 30 petals. Since its introduction the breeder claims that it has remained completely resistant to disease.
Introduced: 1969
Breeder: Sandy, England
Parentage: 'Karl Herbst' x 'Sarabande'

Fragrant Cloud

(syn. Nuage Parfumé, Duftwolke)

Colour: coral-red
Type: Hybrid Tea
Height: 3 feet
Fragrance: strong
This vigorous, upright and spreading bush bears bright coral-red blooms which become geranium-red. However, the flowers are of good form and substance and will open to large double blooms measuring 4-5 inches across, with a strong, rich scent. The dense, glossy foliage is dark green with a copper tint. This is a good rose for beds and borders and for exhibition purposes.
Introduced: 1964
Breeder: Tantau, Germany
Parentage: Seedling x 'Prima Ballerina'

Marlena

Colour: crimson-scarlet
Type: Floribunda
Height: 2-2½ feet
Fragrance: none
Scentless though it is, this rose has an appeal for many gardeners, not only because of the brilliant colour of its flowers, but because its height (or lack of it) makes it ideal for growing at the front of a rose bed or border. Here its branching growth will hide the sometimes ungainly, taller stems of other kinds. It is not only small in stature, but also has small, fairly full blooms and tiny leaves. It flowers freely throughout the season.
Introduced: 1964
Breeder: Kordes, Germany
Parentage: 'Gertrud Westphal' x 'Lilli Marlene'

Fugue

Colour: bright crimson-red
Type: Climber
Height: 10 feet
Fragrance: slight
This is a vigorous plant with abundant dark green, glossy leaves which can be cultivated as a large shrub. Its flowers are semi-double, are of average size and are borne in clusters. It is free-flowering, mainly about early summer, with some recurrent flowering later in the season.
Introduced: 1958
Breeder: Meilland, France
Parentage: 'Alain' x 'Guinée'

Alec's Red

Ena Harkness

Stephen Langdon

Fragrant Cloud

Marlena

Fugue

Topsi

Colour: brilliant, glowing orange-scarlet
Type: Floribunda
Height: 1½-2 feet
Fragrance: slight
This rose is a bushy, compact dwarf with matt, medium-green leaves. Its brilliantly-coloured, very free-flowering flowers are semi-double, having 12 petals. Because of its low height it is particularly useful for planting in small gardens and forward positions in mixed borders.
Introduced: 1971
Breeder: Tantau, Germany
Parentage: 'Fragrant Cloud' x 'Fire Signal'

Evelyn Fison

(syn. Irish Wonder)

Colour: scarlet
Type: Floribunda
Height: 2½ feet
Fragrance: slight
The showy, brilliant scarlet semi-double blooms are carried freely in well-spaced trusses throughout the season. When open they measure up to 3 inches in diameter. They will not fade in bright sunshine, nor are they affected by wet weather. The rich dark green foliage is borne on strong stems and is very resistant to disease. This variety is excellent for bedding purposes.
Introduced: 1962
Breeder: McGredy, N. Ireland
Parentage: 'Moulin Rouge' x 'Korona'

Ernest H. Morse

Colour: crimson
Type: Hybrid Tea
Height: 3 feet
Fragrance: sweet
This is a free-flowering vigorous bush with sturdy upright spreading growth, an excellent bedding variety with good resistance to disease and wet weather. The rich turkey-red double blooms, turning to crimson, are well-formed, carried singly on long stems, and can measure up to 4½ inches across. The dark green leathery foliage is plentiful and contrasts well. This rose is one for the exhibitor's garden, and for arranging.
Introduced: 1964
Breeder: Kordes, Germany
Parentage: 'Brilliant' x 'Prima Ballerina'

Fountain

Colour: rich velvety blood-red
Type: Shrub
Height: 3½ feet
Fragrance: moderate
The growth of this rose is vigorous and upright. Its leaves are red when they are young, but as they mature they become dark green and semi-glossy. Its well-shaped flowers are moderately full (20 petals) and are produced freely both singly and several together. They come into flower earlier than other modern varieties, and repeat well throughout the season.
Introduced: 1972
Breeder: Tantau, Germany
Parentage: not recorded

Lorna Doone

Colour: crimson-scarlet
Type: Floribunda
Height: 2½-3 feet
Fragrance: very slight
The growth of this variety is vigorous and bushy with semi-glossy, dark green leaves. Its crimson flowers are full, with 38 petals, and are borne in trusses. It makes an excellent bedding variety with its brilliant colour.
Introduced: 1972
Breeder: Harkness, England
Parentage: 'Red Dandy' x 'Lilli Marlene'

Mister Lincoln

Colour: dark crimson
Type: Hybrid Tea
Height: 3-4 feet
Fragrance: rich
Many crimson roses are renowned for their fragrance. This fairly new variety is no exception for the dark crimson blooms, flushed with scarlet, are very strongly scented. The blooms are very large, full of petals and well-shaped. The foliage is dark green, the growth vigorous; light pruning gives a bush about 4 feet tall.
It was an All-America Rose Selection in 1968.
Introduced: 1964
Breeder: Swim and Weeks, U.S.A.
Parentage: 'Chrysler Imperial' x 'Charles Mallerin'

Topsi

Evelyn Fison

Ernest H. Morse

Fountain

Lorna Doone

Mister Lincoln

59

Gustav Frahm

Colour: crimson-scarlet
Type: Floribunda Shrub
Height: 3½ feet
Fragrance: slight
The semi-double flowers open flat in a rosette formation and are borne in large tight trusses of crimson-scarlet with darker shading towards the edges. The blooms are fairly rain-resistant but they tend to lose their brightness with age. However, they are very plentiful during the summer and autumn. The growth is very vigorous with an abundance of light green foliage, and will stand up to wind and weather, although it may be necessary to watch for mildew.
Introduced: 1958
Breeder: Kordes, Germany
Parentage: 'Fanal' x 'Ama'

Red Devil

(syn. Coeur d'Amour)

Colour: scarlet
Type: Hybrid Tea
Height: 3½ feet
Fragrance: strong
This variety produces excellent blooms for the exhibitor. The large, full-petalled flowers, borne on strong stems, are perfectly shaped with high pointed centres and are a bright scarlet with lighter reverse. In damp, cloudy weather the blooms have a tendency to 'ball'. The vigorous upright growth is well covered with leathery, glossy medium-green foliage.
Introduced: 1967
Breeder: Dickson, N. Ireland
Parentage: 'Silver Lining' x 'Prima Ballerina'

City of Belfast

Colour: bright orange
Type: Floribunda
Height: 2-2½ feet
Fragrance: slight
Though this colour is somewhat difficult to associate with other colours, it has become popular in recent years. 'City of Belfast' is one of the best of its colour range and it has won a number of awards. The blooms are medium-sized, borne in clusters on compact plants which make the variety excellent for bedding purposes. The shining foliage is tinged with red when it first opens.
Introduced: 1968
Breeder: McGredy, N. Ireland
Parentage: 'Evelyn Fison' x (Circus' x 'Korona')

Henry Nevard

Colour: crimson-scarlet
Type: Hybrid Perpetual
Height: 4-5 feet
Fragrance: strong
This is a vigorous variety which grows into a sturdy, upright bushy Shrub with dark green, leathery leaves. It has very large, double, crimson-scarlet flowers, which are cupped in shape and have about 30 petals. It flowers recurrently through the season.
Introduced: 1924
Breeder: Cant, England
Parentage: Unknown

Berlin

Colour: orange-scarlet
Type: Modern Shrub
Height: 5 feet
Fragrance: slight
It is a vigorous rose, which makes an excellent specimen bush. Its foliage is light green. It has single flowers with golden stamens. They have 5-7 petals which are 3 inches in diameter.
The blooms are produced in clusters. It is very free-flowering and has been found to be healthy.
Introduced: 1949
Breeder: Kordes, Germany
Parentage: 'Eva' x 'Peace'

Rosa Moyesii 'Geranium'

Colour: geranium-red
Type: variety of Species
Height: 8-10 feet
Fragrance: slight
Rosa moyesii itself, introduced into cultivation from China in 1894, is always remembered for its reddish-crimson single blooms which are followed by large bottle-shaped hips. It is a vigorous Shrub, often growing 12 feet tall. 'Geranium' is less vigorous, but equally spectacular around midsummer and for some weeks afterwards, and the hips are even larger than those of its parent. The leaflets are small and dark green. Little pruning is needed.
Parentage: Sport or seedling from *R. moyesii*

Gustav Frahm

Red Devil

City of Belfast

Henry Nevard

Berlin

Rosa Moyesii 'Geranium'

Kronenbourg

(syn. Flaming Peace)

Colour: red to crimson fading to purple with old gold reverse
Type: Hybrid Tea
Height: 4 feet
Fragrance: very slight
This grows to a tall and sturdy bush that has the vigour and growing habit of its parent, 'Peace'. Its flowers are moderately full, with about 25 petals and large. Its form makes it an excellent exhibition rose. It appears to be quite hardy.
Introduced: 1965
Breeder: McGredy, N. Ireland
Parentage: Sport from 'Peace'

Chianti

Colour: purplish-maroon
Type: Shrub
Height: 5 feet
Fragrance: very strong
This rose grows as a well-formed bush. Its leaves are semi-glossy and medium to light green in colour. Its blood-red flowers are produced with very great freedom in one display and have a charming formality. When they are first open the petals are cupped, but later they become reflexed. The blooms are very full with over 40 petals.
Introduced: 1965
Breeder: Austin, England
Parentage: *R. gallica* 'Cardinal de Richelieu' x 'Dusky Maiden'

Souvenir du Dr Jamain

Colour: rich, dark, wine-crimson
Type: Hybrid Perpetual
Height: 6 feet
Fragrance: strong
This is not a very vigorous rose. Its leaves are dark green and it produces large, orange-red hips. Its flowers are full, have about 40 petals and are 3-3½ inches across. Its main flowering time is from late spring to early summer with some repeat flowering later in the summer. To grow really well it needs good soil and preferably a westerly aspect. If it is trained up a wall, it will reach 10 feet high.
Introduced: 1865
Breeder: Lacharme, France
Parentage: 'Charles Lefébvre' seedling

Park Jewel

Colour: blood-red
Type: Moss
Height: 5 feet
Fragrance: very strong
This rose is an upright, bushy grower. It is free-flowering and blooms late in the season. It has large, full flowers, having about 35 petals. The blooms are globular in form and have a diameter of 3 inches. They are borne in clusters of up to five. Its foliage is leathery, wrinkled and light green in colour.
Introduced: 1956
Breeder: Kordes, Germany
Parentage: 'Independence' x a red Moss rose

Roger Lambelin

Colour: deep crimson, margined and streaked with white
Type: Hybrid Perpetual
Height: 4 feet
Fragrance: moderate
This rose is a moderately vigorous grower but has rather weak stalks. The foliage is dark green. Its flowers are large and full with about 35 petals. They are fringed at their edges, giving them an unusual carnation-like effect. It is free-flowering in summer with a few blooms later. This is a rather difficult rose to grow and requires good soil. Although generally healthy, it has a tendency to be affected by mildew.
Introduced: 1890
Breeder: Schwartz, France
Parentage: Sport from 'Fisher Holmes'

Rosa x Pruhoniciana

(syn. R. 'Hillieri')

Colour: very dark crimson
Type: Species
Height: 9-10 feet
Fragrance: slight
This very vigorous rose grows into a tall bush with graceful arching branches. It has small, attractive leaves and produces dark red, narrow, bottle-shaped hips. The flowers are single, with 5-7 petals, and are seen at their best when the sun shines through their rich colourful petals. It is necessary to guard this variety against mildew.
Introduced: 1924
Breeder: Hillier, England
Parentage: *R. willmottiae* x *R. moyesii*

Kronenbourg

Chianti

Souvenir du Dr Jamain

Park Jewel

Roger Lambelin

Rosa x Pruhoniciana

63

Care and Cultivation of Roses

Selecting and ordering It is important to order your roses early in the season, that is between June and August, when most of the rose shows are held. During this period the roses may be seen in flower at the nurseries and by ordering promptly you can be sure of the most popular varieties being available.

It is advisable to order from a rose specialist, and from one who buds his own plants, rather than from a man who is not a producer. This is because the grower selling under his own name has a reputation to maintain, and no well-known rose specialist can afford to sell plants which do not give satisfaction. When you visit the nursery, or display garden adjoining it, watch for the habit of growth, disease and weather resistance and freedom of flowering of any of the species provisionally selected.

There is a great deal of variation in the quality of maiden rose plants supplied from various sources, and cheap offers are often the dearest in the long run, as the quality is normally very inferior. Bearing in mind that a healthy rose, when once properly planted, may last from 12 to 20 years or more, with reasonable treatment, it is false economy to attempt to save a few shillings on the initial cost when this may mean the difference between success and failure. It is essential to obtain plants from a reliable source. This is because of the need for them to be hardy and well-ripened, true to name, budded on a suitable rootstock which will transplant readily and not sucker freely and free from disease spores.

Bare root roses are sometimes still on offer in overheated departmental stores, but nowadays these are normally offered packed in individual polythene bags. The trouble with these roses is that they are frequently subjected to this overheated atmosphere for considerable periods, with consequent dehydration showing in bone-dry roots and shrivelled stems. A rose purchased in this condition is unlikely to flourish unless measures are taken to plump up the wood again by burying the entire plant for about ten days in moist soil, before planting it in its permanent quarters. Another disadvantage of these pre-packaged roses is that each package acts as a miniature greenhouse, and the stems are forced into tender premature growth while they are awaiting sale. This tender growth receives a severe check when the plants are taken out of their packages and exposed to the hazards of the open garden.

Container-grown roses are offered at many nurseries and garden centres. These enable the planting season to be extended throughout the year, as no root disturbance should occur in plant-

1 When Roses are purchased in containers for planting from autumn to early spring, the growths should be cut back to within a few inches of ground level.
2 Slitting the container after the hole has been dug to receive the plant.
3 The roots should be spread out and fine soil worked among them before the soil is firmed with the feet.

ing from containers into the permanent beds. They may even be planted when in full bloom without any damage to the appearance or health of the plant.
Soil Ordinary well-drained soil which has grown good crops of vegetables will suit most roses. It should be slightly acid (pH 5.5 to 6.5) but if the soil is very acid or alkaline, some special treatment will be necessary. (See pages 73 and 74.)

Perfect drainage is vitally important. The soil that is just right for roses is medium loam, because it is crumbly and the particles allow free drainage and aeration of the roots. Light soil is composed of large particles through which water freely runs, while in heavy soil the particles are very small and water trickles through much more slowly; if it is above a fairly hard pan of subsoil the top-soil is likely to become waterlogged. This means you need to give the light soil a greater ability to retain water and thus slow up its run-through rate, and to increase the speed of passage through the heavier soil by making its small particles stick together and form rather larger units artificially. Both objects can be achieved by adding humus-making material when the bed is prepared.

When double digging, a layer of chopped turf should be laid face down in the bottom of the trench. Then a reasonable amount (less on heavy soils) of well-decomposed garden compost or animal manure should be added to the lower spit. The top spit will be improved in generally poor soil by adding granulated peat, compost and bonemeal (at the rate of 4 ounces per square yard) and hoof and horn meal (at 2 ounces per square yard). These should be thoroughly mixed with the soil and not left on the surface or in layers.

If the soil is heavy clay it can usually be broken down and rendered suitable for roses by rough digging over and incorporating gypsum or hydrated lime at the rate of 3 pounds per square yard. On heavy land the beds should be raised a few inches above the general level, but sunk slightly on sandy soil.

Planting This may be done safely from late October to the end of March whenever the soil is friable and free from frost. Autumn planting usually gives the best results, provided the soil is not too wet for planting firmly; otherwise it will be better to wait for

suitable conditions. On receipt of the bushes they should be heeled in temporarily in a trench, throwing plenty of soil over the roots and treading firmly. When the soil in the bed is friable, a large bucket of moist granulated peat, into which a couple of handfuls of meat and bonemeal have been mixed, should be prepared. The position of each bush in the bed is marked with a stick. Distance apart will depend on the vigour and habit of the variety, but on an average soil about 18 inches each way will be about right for most. Exceptionally vigorous kinds, such as 'Peace', which need light pruning, may be better at least 2 feet apart. The roots should be soaked for a couple of hours before planting. A shallow hole is taken out wide enough to take roots when fully spread. The plant should be inspected carefully for suckers emerging from the

---

1 When preparing to plant Roses mark out the area to show the positions.
2 Take out one hole at a time deep enough to ensure that the union of stock and scion is at soil level.
3 Spread out the roots.
4 Fill the hole with fine soil and work it well round the roots.
5 Firm the area around the bush and cut back the growth to a few inches.
6 A stout stake is inserted in the ground before planting a standard Rose.

---

root system, and any found should be pulled off. Damaged and broken roots must be trimmed and unripe or damaged shoots removed, also all leaves and flower buds. The prepared plant is then tested in the hole for correct depth; the union of the stock and scion should be just covered with soil. A few handfuls of the peat mixture are thrown over and between the roots and the hole half filled with fine soil and trodden firmly before filling up to the correct level. Standard roses are staked before covering the roots to avoid possible injury. It is beneficial to mulch new beds with 2 inches of granulated peat, to conserve moisture.

Watering Without enough water, plants cannot absorb fertilisers from the soil and the many complex plant functions cannot be sustained. Copious watering of roses at all times during the growing season when rainfall is inadequate is imperative. It is best not to wet the foliage because this might encourage disease, or the blooms because they might become blemished. An effective method is to weave an upturned, perforated hose among the bushes so that the water penetrates down into the soil.

Pruning All dead or decadent wood should be cut out as soon as it is noticed at any time. Full-scale pruning should be done when the bushes are dormant, or nearly so. This may be done at any

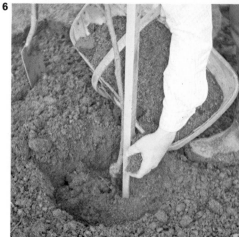

1

2

3

4

5

6

time from January to mid-March, depending on the weather and the area. In the first spring after planting all groups, except climbing sports of hybrid tea roses, should have weak or twiggy shoots removed entirely, together with any sappy growth. The remainder should be cut back just above a dormant shoot bud pointing away from the centre of the plant and not more than 6 inches from the base. Spring planted roses may be pruned in the hand just before planting. Climbing sports of hybrid teas should just be tipped and the main shoots bent over by securing the ends to canes or wires, to force the lower buds into growth. On light hungry soils it may be advisable not to prune any groups the first year, but to encourage as much new growth as possible by mulching and watering.

1 The head of a standard Rose before pruning with twiggy and dead wood.
2 After pruning, when the growth has been tidied up.
3 The pruning of climbing Roses varies with the group to which they belong, but dormant buds can be encouraged to grow by cutting back the laterals.
4 Pruning a newly-planted climbing Rose by shortening the long growths.
5 Pruning a newly-planted bush Rose by cutting the growth down to within a few inches of ground level.

1

2

4

3

5

1 An overgrown rambler Rose much in need of pruning.
2 Dead shoots are cut away, together with old flowered growths and very thin, unwanted shoots. The work is best carried out in late summer immediately after flowering is over.
3 Cutting down the old canes.

Subsequent years Pruning of hybrid teas may be hard, moderate or light, according to circumstances. Light pruning is generally preferable on poor sandy soils which do not encourage a lot of new wood. This means cutting back new shoots formed in the previous season to about two-thirds of their length and removing all weak or twiggy growth. On average soils moderate pruning may be done, involving cutting back all new wood about half way and removing entirely the weak and twiggy shoots. Hard pruning is seldom necessary for modern varieties, but some will respond to it on a good soil with ample feeding. It requires the cutting out of all but two or three of the main growths and reducing these to just above a dormant bud about 6 inches from the base.

Floribundas require different treatment. The object is to ensure as continuous a display of colour during the season as possible. This requires the application of a differential pruning system, based on the age of the wood. Growth produced from the base in the previous season should merely be shortened to the first convenient bud below the old flower truss. The laterals on two-year-old wood should be cut back half way and any three-year-old wood cut hard back to about three eyes from the base. As with all groups, all dead, decadent, unripe and twiggy wood should be removed entirely.

Shrub roses and the old garden roses in general do not require much pruning. Apart from the cutting out of dead and exhausted wood and cutting back a main growth near the base occasionally to encourage new basal growth, pruning is mainly confined to remedying overcrowding and ensuring a shapely outline.

The treatment of climbers varies with the group to which they belong. Generally, the more recurrent flowering the variety, the less rampant is its growth and the less the pruning required. The once-flowering wichuraiana ramblers, which renew themselves with new canes from the base each season after flowering, should have all old flowering wood cut out and the new canes tied in to take its place. Climbing sports of hybrid teas and other climbing hybrid teas require little pruning, but should be trained fanwise or horizontally to force as many dormant eyes into growth as possible. Flowers are borne either on laterals or sub-laterals. Recurrent flowering pillar roses, such as 'Aloha', 'Coral

1

3

2

4

1 The new canes are tied in carefully.
2 Rambling Roses can be trained horizontally over beds to provide a good cover. The long growths are tied down to pegs in the ground.
3 Removing dead flowerheads.
4 A complete rose fertiliser should be applied during April.

Removal of spent flowers is essential if a later crop is to be produced and seed pods should never be allowed to develop. Dead-heading should be a routine operation throughout the season. In the first summer after planting merely the flower and foot of the stalk, without any leaves, should be removed, but in subsequent years the growth from the pruning point may be reduced to half way, to ensure a fine second display. Disbudding will also be necessary for the keen exhibitor and those who insist on high quality blooms. Not more than three buds are left on hybrid tea stems for garden display or a single bud for exhibition. In the autumn any long growths should be shortened to minimise possible gale damage.

Feeding Before embarking on a feeding programme you should find out whether your soil is naturally acid or alkaline. There are a number of soil-testing kits available. Lime, if required, is best applied in the form of ground chalk (calcium carbonate) during the early winter months, at 3 or 4 ounces per square yard, sprinkled evenly over the surface of the beds and left for the winter rains to wash it down. By the time the spring mulch is due, the lime should have done its work. As roses prefer a

Dawn' and 'Parade', require only the removal of dead or exhausted wood and any which is weak or twiggy, plus sufficient thinning out of the remaining wood to avoid overcrowding.

General cultivation Suckers must be removed before they grow large. They may come from any point below the inserted bud and with standards they may appear either on the standard stem below the head or anywhere on the root system. The roots of roses should not be disturbed any more than is essential to the removal of weeds and suckers.

Where light or moderate pruning is practised, summer thinning or de-shooting may be necessary, and this will be routine procedure for the keen exhibitor. All side shoots appearing before the terminal buds have opened should be pinched out as soon as they are large enough to handle. While watering is not a practical proposition on a large scale, newly planted roses may need the roots soaking thoroughly at weekly intervals during hot weather. Roses planted in dry positions, against walls or close-boarded fences, will also require regular watering in the summer.

slightly acid soil, it may be necessary to apply lime every year, though never on chalky soil.

During February and March it is beneficial to apply a dressing of meat and bonemeal at 4 ounces per square yard, pricking it just below the surface. If this proves difficult to obtain in small quantities sterilised bonemeal may be used instead. About the middle of April a complete rose fertiliser can be applied to established beds, according to the makers' instructions. There are many of these available, or a useful compound fertiliser may be made up quite cheaply from 16 parts of superphosphate of lime, 10 parts of sulphate of potash, 5 parts of sulphate of ammonia, 2 parts of sulphate of magnesia (commercial Epsom Salts) and 2 parts of sulphate of iron. These parts are in terms of weight, and the ingredients must be mixed thoroughly, any lumps being crushed. The fertiliser should be sprinkled evenly at about a *level* tablespoonful per plant, afterwards hoeing and watering in if necessary. The temptation to use a double dose in the hope of obtaining spectacular results should be resisted.

Alternatively, for those who do not wish to go to much trouble, many firms market a rose fertiliser to the well-known 'Tonks' formula, which was based originally on the chemical analysis of the ashes of a complete rose tree

1 Peat used as a summer mulch round rose bushes to conserve moisture.
2 Peat being worked into the soil prior to planting Roses.
3 Around the middle of May a mulch of animal manure is applied.

after burning it in a crucible. The formula comprises 12 parts of superphosphate of lime, 10 parts of nitrate of potash, 8 parts of sulphate of lime, 2 parts of sulphate of magnesia and 1 part of sulphate of iron. It should be applied at the rate of 3 or 4 ounces per square yard and pricked in with a border fork.

About the middle of May, when the soil will have started to warm up, a mulch of animal manure or, if this is unobtainable, compost, granulated peat,

leafmould or spent hops should be applied evenly to the beds, preferably 2 inches deep. If peat, leafmould or spent hops are used they should be well moistened and fortified with a further application of the compound rose fertiliser, at the same rate as in mid-April. It is a good plan to wash this in with a hose jet applied at pressure to the mulch. The keen grower, with ambitions to produce excellent specimen blooms, may wish to try liquid stimulants from the stage of bud formation. Apart from liquid animal manures, which should *always* be applied in very dilute form (no stronger than a pale straw colour) and at intervals of ten days or so, soot water and soluble blood are useful nitrogenous fertilisers. Nitrate of potash (at $\frac{1}{2}$ ounce per gallon) and superphosphate of lime (at 1 ounce per gallon) may also be used safely at these strengths. The important points to watch in liquid feeding are: to use the feed in very dilute form only; to ensure that there is already plenty of moisture in the soil before applying and to discontinue application at the end of July.

About the end of August, especially in a wet season, it is a good plan to apply a dressing of sulphate of potash to the rose beds at the rate of 3 ounces per square yard. This will help to ripen and harden the wood in readiness for the winter. It should be pricked in along with what

remains of the mid-May mulch.

Pests Rose pests should be tackled in the early stages before damage becomes widespread. Common pests include caterpillars of all types, the rose slugworm sawfly and leaf rolling sawfly.

Caterpillars These cause the familiar 'holed' appearance of leaves and indented leaf edges. Both leaves and stems should be sprayed with an approved insecticide from early May onwards, as soon as the first symptoms of caterpillar attacks appear.

Rose slugworm sawfly The leaves take on a skeletonised appearance, which is the result of feeding by the yellowish larvae on the green leaf tissue. They are controlled by spraying in the same way as caterpillars.

Leaf rolling sawfly The leaves become rolled downwards and inwards. The maggot feeds on the tissue inside the rolled leaf. Pressing these leaves and then pulling them off and burning them seems to be the only fully effective treatment, but encouraging results can be obtained by spraying with trichlorphon at least three times between mid-May and mid-June.

Tortrix moth The leaves folded inward show the presence of the larva, which may be brownish or green. Pressing the folded leaves between the finger and thumb, and then pulling them off and burning them is the only really effective treatment.

Shoot borer sawfly The tip of a young shoot will sometimes wilt, though lower down the growth seems healthy. The brownish maggot of this sawfly bores down inside the shoot, feeding on the pith. Pressure applied just below the drooping tip will often cause the maggot to wriggle out backwards. Growing points should be sprayed or dusted with an approved insecticide from early May at fortnightly intervals.

Chafer Beetle Typical damage consists of flower buds eaten on one side only in early summer. The larvae feed on the rose roots in light soils, especially in the Home Counties. Top growth should be sprayed regularly as soon as the first symptoms are noticed. Where the damage is extensive, an appropriate insecticide should be forked into the soil near the bushes to a depth of 6 inches to destroy the larvae.

Rose leafhopper Pale mottled areas on leaves in May and June are caused by the small yellowish nymphs sucking the sap. The undersides of leaves and the soil beneath should be sprayed early in May with malathion or gamma-BHC.

Greenfly The familiar colonies are to be seen on tender growing points of young

1 Rose Slugworm Sawfly larvae, and the damage caused by them.
2 The distinctive mottling of the leaves of Roses attacked by Rose Leafhopper.
3 Aphids, or Greenfly, are the commonest pests of Roses.

1 The pale green Capsid Bug causes punctures on and distortion of Rose leaves, as well as browning of the buds.
2 A Cuckoo Spit Insect emerging from the frothy 'spit' deposited on the leaf.
3 Powdery mildew, a disease of Roses.

shoots, on the undersides of leaves and below the flower buds and on the footstalks. They suck the sap and multiply at an alarming rate. Any of the proprietary contact sprays, other than DDT, may be used, applying with a mist-like spray to ensure full coverage over both surfaces of leaves. A follow-up spray should be applied about three days later.

Thrips Early flowers may develop with blackened or stained petal edges, presenting a withered or scorched appearance. Leaves may also be mottled and marbled. Foliage, buds and opening flowers are best sprayed in May with either derris or malathion.

Capsid bug Withered young flower buds and punctured and distorted foliage, sometimes with brown areas round the punctures, show the presence of nymphs of the green capsid bug. They are active and drop to the soil or hide beneath a leaf at the first sign of danger. Early in the season the growing points, foliage and soil beneath the plants should be sprayed with gamma-BHC (Lindane) or dusted with pyrethrum extract.

Cuckoo spit insect (frog hopper) The yellowish-green nymphs conceal themselves inside the frothy 'spit', usually found at the leaf axils, and suck the sap. A coarse spray applied at pressure, using derris, pyrethrum or malathion, controls them.

Diseases The three main rose diseases are black spot, rust and mildew. The first two will rarely affect roses grown in industrial or built-up areas.

Powdery mildew This disease may affect

gallon of water). Any leaves which have fallen on the beds should be raked up and burnt during the winter.

Rose rust This is the most serious rose disease, but fortunately the spores seem unable to flourish in industrial and built-up areas. The disease may be identified by the orange coloured pustules (uredospores) appearing on the undersides of the leaves from June onwards; these show as yellow patches on the upper surface. Later in the season the over-wintering teleutospores are produced. These are black, thick-walled spores which remain on the undersides of the leaves or winter on the wood and carry the disease forward to the following season. The thread-like mycelium of the fungus beneath the bark of shoots will also carry the disease over, and in advanced cases vertical cracks will appear in the wood which will have a scarred appearance.

As with black spot preventive spraying is the only effective control. Just after pruning, the dormant wood should be sprayed with a copper preparation, such as Bordeaux mixture. When the leaves are unfolding and following this at about fortnightly intervals, and also after heavy rain, protective spraying with maneb or zineb, at the rate of ¾ ounce per gallon of soft water, will be necessary in gardens where rust has been troublesome before. The leaves should be well covered with the solution, paying particular attention to the underneath. Leaves showing the orange-coloured pustules should be removed and burnt, as should any fallen leaves.

Some rose problems solved

Weeds Light regular hoeing is a most effective way of keeping rose beds free of weeds but, for the less energetic, there are two excellent but undoubtedly rather more expensive ways of doing the same job. These consist in putting down chemicals. There are two types of weed-killers, or herbicides as they are called. The first is based on paraquat and di-quat. A solution of this, made up to the maker's instructions, is watered on to the weeds during the growing season when they are in leaf. Prevent it falling on the lower leaves of the rose bushes by applying it from a sprinkler bar attached to a watering can. Another chemical, simazine, is applied in the late winter after all growing weeds have been cleared. After it has been put on, the soil should be left undisturbed. It acts by preventing the weed seedling leaves from emerging through the surface of the soil.

Very alkaline soil This is generally indicated by the fact that the subsoil is chalk or there are small pieces of chalk in it. To remedy this situation, first double dig the ground and mix in copious quantities of humus-making material such as garden compost. Then allow the soil to stand during the winter. Finally, if time allows, sow a crop of

1 Black Spot is a disease of Roses caused by the fungus Diplocarpon rosae. 2 The disease known as Rose Rust may affect both leaves and stems.

all areas. Roses planted in a dry spot or in a draughty bed between two houses, or near a brick wall or a dense hedge seem particularly prone to the disease. It is a surface fungus only, which does not invade the tissue of the leaf. Spraying the upper and under surfaces of the leaves at the first sign with a recognised mildew specific will control the disease, or a dilute solution of washing soda (1 ounce of crystals to 1 gallon of soft water, together with a little liquid soap to act as a spreader) may be used instead.

Black spot In rural areas black spot seems to be present in greater or lesser degree every season. Once the black spots have appeared, that leaf cannot be cured. The spots have fringed edges, are quite black and gradually increase in size until several may merge to form a completely black area of irregular shape. The remainder of the leaf turns yellow and is shed prematurely. This disease is controlled by regular preventive spraying, which provides a protective coating over the leaf surface. Maneb 80 and captan preparations, such as orthocide or zineb, are mostly favoured nowadays and should be made up exactly to the makers' instructions. Picking off and burning leaves bearing the ominous black spots in the early stages will help to control the disease, but preventive spraying at fortnightly intervals, avoiding overcrowding, and proper pruning are the best answer. Trees which have suffered from a severe attack should be pruned fairly hard the following winter and sprayed with copper sulphate solution (1 ounce of copper sulphate to 1

mustard seed and dig the crop in next spring.

Very acid soil Over-acid soil is often sandy and peaty and is indicated by many heathland plants growing wild in the district. It needs added lime. It is difficult for an amateur to calculate the amount because it varies with the condition of the soil, so it is better to get expert advice. (You can test for pH value with cheap testing kits, available at horticultural stores.)

Clay and waterlogging We have already talked about breaking down heavy clay soil. Sometimes such ground becomes waterlogged and, as well as double digging, you will have to drain it. A simple but often effective way of doing this is to dig a trench about 18 inches deep across the centre of the bed and fill it with nine inches of small stones or sharp sand, covering this with some brushwood or perforated polythene and refilling the trench with top soil (see diagram). It is a good idea to raise the height of the bed about six inches above the surrounding ground.

Rose sick soil When roses have been growing in a bed for more than ten years, do not replace them with new ones because they will not flourish. The soil has become 'rose sick' and needs attention. This can be overcome in a number of ways. Either cut a new bed elsewhere or replace the soil to a depth of about 18 inches with new soil, which has not been used for roses.

Alternatively green manure with mustard seed as for very alkaline soils. Or, if only a few roses need replacing, dig a hole for each, 18 inches across and 18 inches deep, and fill with fresh soil. Container-grown roses are particularly good for such situations because you can stand them on a layer of fresh soil at the bottom of the hole and pack the space around them with soil.

Severe frost Bush roses will stand quite low temperatures without danger. Icy winds will damage standards, so if they are in very exposed positions, tie straw or bracken around their heads. Take it off as soon as the danger passes so that there is no premature growth. This applies to temperate zones but in some places in Canada and North America, where the climate is extreme, it may be necessary to mound up your bushes and lift your standards and bury them for the winter.

Heavy rain Heavy rain can loosen bushes and form a pocket in the soil at their base. This can fill with water, which is likely to freeze and damage the union. Deal with this by regular inspection and treading in.

High winds Heavy gales loosen roses and disturb the roots. Cutting back bush roses late in autumn is a good prevention. In addition, see that all stakes and other supports of standard and climbing roses are kept in good order and that the ties are sound.

Drought Give copious amounts of water as under-watering will only encourage the roots to come to the surface.

Roses that sprawl Hybrid tea and floribunda roses that send out almost horizontal shoots and get entangled with their neighbours are unsightly. You can deal with this by pruning offending shoots at an upward-growing bud.

Blind shoots Sometimes, particularly after a late spring, roses send out shoots which look as though they will flower but, in fact, carry no buds. If left these will break naturally, but flowering can be expedited by cutting back to an outward-pointing bud well down the stem.

Climbers bare at their bases Quite frequently climbing roses, particularly the sports, become bare at their base. If this happens, untie the plant in the spring and lay it out horizontally on the ground for a few weeks. This allows the sap to go to the lower buds instead of rushing to the upper ones. When signs of activity appear, re-tie the climber. If you want to cheat, you can plant a bush rose at its base. This will at least conceal the ugliness.

Shrub roses bare at their bases The best way to deal with these is to cut one or two stems back each year to an outward-growing bud about one foot above the ground. Although it is unnecessarily drastic, climbers can be treated in the same way.

Shrivelled leaves New leaves sometimes become discoloured and shrivelled in the spring. This is almost sure to be due to cold winds and occasional frosts and not to disease.

Propagating *Seed* Roses may be raised from seed, but as modern hybrid teas and floribundas have such a complex ancestry, they do not come true, and the vast majority of seedlings will be inferior to their parents. Raising from seed is usually only done by raisers of new varieties, who deliberately cross two selected parents under controlled conditions. Nevertheless there is nothing very difficult about raising roses from seed. People often express surprise that it is quite easy to have a rose in flower in three months after sowing the seed. The great difficulty is not to flower rose seedlings, but to raise a really good one of commercial value.

Many of the cluster-flowered groups will provide a source of interest to amateurs interested in growing from seed. Three groups which are recommended for the beginner are the Pemberton hybrid musks, the hybrid rugosas and the miniature roses, the seed of which is sometimes offered under the heading of 'Fairy Roses'. The heps (or hips) may be gathered as late in the autumn as is safe before severe frosts, usually up to mid-October, and stored under cover in a box or a flower pot filled with a mixture of moist peat and sand or just sand until March. Then rub them between the palms of the hands,

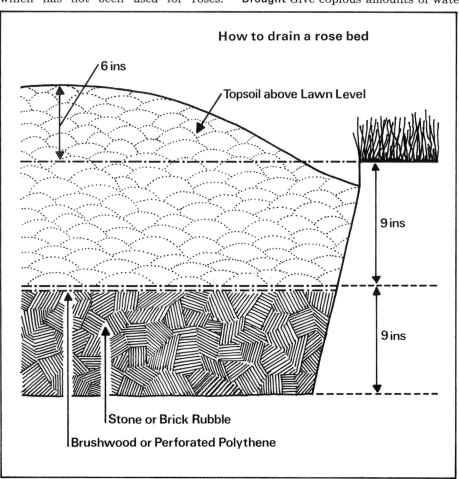

How to drain a rose bed

6 ins

Topsoil above Lawn Level

9 ins

9 ins

Stone or Brick Rubble

Brushwood or Perforated Polythene

3

4

when you will find that the seeds will separate from the pulp. The seed may be sown in March in pots, seed pans or boxes of good compost—say John Innes No 1. They should be spaced 1 inch apart each way and covered with ½ inch of soil, finishing off with a sprinkling of sharp sand. A high temperature is not desirable —between 50° and 60°F (10–16°C) is about right. Germination is irregular and uncertain and the individual seedlings may be transferred to thumb pots when one true leaf has developed. Some will flower on tiny plants before the end of June and may be transplanted outside if of attractive colouring.

An alternative method, just as easy, is

Rose hips are prepared for seed sowing by stratification in pots.
1 Placing Rose hips on moist sand.
2 A further layer of sand is added.
3 The sand is firmed by hand.
4 A cross-section showing the hips.

to sow the seed in shallow drills out of doors, applying a dressing of moist granulated peat to the surface to avoid too rapid drying out of the soil. Some of the seedlings will not flower until the second or third season, and these usually develop a climbing habit.

Cuttings These may be taken of the stronger groups, notably the wichuraiana ramblers, some of the old shrub

roses and the most vigorous floribundas. Ripe growths of the current season are selected in September, shortened to 9 inches by rejecting unripe ends and all but two leaves at the top are removed. The cuttings thus prepared are placed upright in a narrow trench, about 6 inches deep, to which coarse sand has been added. The trench is filled in and the cuttings made firm, leaving the top 3 inches above the surface. They are left undisturbed for at least the whole of the following season, apart from watering and weeding, as necessary. Layering may also be successfully employed with the stronger growing climbing, rambling and shrub types.

Budding or grafting roses Some of the most vigorous hybrid teas and floribundas may be grown on their own roots from cuttings, but most roses make better plants, and in a shorter time, when budded or grafted on a suitable rootstock. There is a range of such stocks used, mostly species or selected strains of such. In this country the seedling briar *(R. canina)* is the most popular, as it thrives on most soils, transplants well, has a long life and is hardy. There are also many selected strains of *R. canina* used to ensure greater uniformity or comparative freedom from thorns or other characteristics, as well as *R. multiflora* and *R. rugosa,* the latter being largely used for standard rose stems.

Budding is carried out in early summer when the sap is running freely in both rootstock and cultivar. For bush and climbing forms a 'T' cut is made in the bark of the stock at or about soil level, with the vertical cut not more than an inch long. The two flaps of bark are then carefully raised with the handle of the budding knife, to enable a shoot bud of the selected cultivar, suitably prepared on its own shield of bark, to be pushed down behind the flaps to the bottom of the cut, so that the bud faces outwards. The top of the shield of bark on the bud is then trimmed flush with the top of the 'T' cut and the bud tied in securely with raffia or fastened with a plastic tie.

The preparation of the shield of bark, carrying an 'eye' or shoot bud, is the part which usually causes most difficulty. This must be in the correct stage of development—not too ripe and not immature. Usually a stem carrying a terminal flower which is just about ready to shed its petals will provide suitable material. The stem should be cut about 8 or 9 inches below the flower, and the flower and footstalk cut away, leaving the stem with perhaps three leaves. The leaves are cut off about half an inch from the main stem, leaving this length of leaf stalk to facilitate handling of the bud, which may be identified as a tiny nob at the angle between the stalk and the main stem. There will then be three buds, each with half an inch of stalk attached, and the centre bud of these three is most likely to be in the right stage of development.

The object is to remove the bud with a shield of bark about 1 inch long with the bud as its centre, without cutting so deeply into the wood that the bud is injured in the process of removing the piece of wood behind it. It is best to use a special budding knife, which has a single blade and a smooth bone handle which tapers to a point at the end, this point being used for lifting the bark of the rootstock before inserting the bud on its shield. Starting half an inch above the bud make a cut gradually going deeper so that it is deepest just behind the bud. Then reduce the depth so that the knife blade emerges about half an

1 A T-cut is made in the stock with a sharp budding knife.
2 The bud is prepared and the pith removed from behind the bud of the scion.
3 The prepared bud is slipped into place behind the two flaps of the T-shaped cut, and pushed firmly down to join securely.
4 The union is bound with tape.

inch beyond the bud. There will then be a boat-shaped piece of bark carrying an eye or shoot bud, with a small piece of stalk attached and with a thin slice of wood behind the bark and the bud. This wood must be removed without injuring the bud, and this is best done in two

stages. Holding the shield with the thumb nail of one hand pressed hard against the wood behind the bud, with the first finger and thumb of the other hand separate the wood and bark above the bud, using the blade of the knife to give a start. A sudden sideways snatch will remove this wood without damaging the bud, which is protected by the thumbnail of the other hand. Reverse the shield and proceed similarly with the other half, and then trim the base of the shield flat with a cross cut, ready for insertion behind the bark of the rootstock.

All of this may sound rather involved, but with a little practice it becomes automatic. Speed is essential to a successful union, as the cambium layer is very thin and must not be allowed to dry—otherwise failure is certain.

If the shield and the bud remain green, nothing more is done until the following February, when the whole of the top growth is cut away immediately above the inserted bud, which should start to grow in late March or April. In the one season this will make the maiden plant as sold by the rose nurseryman.

Standard roses are formed by inserting two or three buds in the main stem of rugosa stocks at the desired height, or in the case of canina stems, into two or three laterals of the current season's growth. All non-budded growth is removed in the following February and the budded laterals shortened to about 6 inches. The maiden growth will need tying to small canes as it develops, or pinching back to reduce the need for staking and to encourage a bushy head.

Grafting, as distinct from budding, which is a form of shield grafting, is normally done under glass and is often resorted to by nurserymen in order to work up a stock of a new variety.

Simple hybridisation New commercial varieties are produced by the cross-pollination of two chosen parents under carefully controlled conditions. The resultant seeds are sown and grown on. The weather in this country is such that it is wiser to make the cross in a greenhouse, so that the hips or seed pods will become sufficiently ripe before the cold weather.

Much thought is devoted to the choice of parents. The seed parent must be a variety which sets seeds freely, and one that flowers at the same time as the chosen pollen parent—otherwise it may not be possible to make the cross at all. Such qualities as freedom of flowering, disease resistance, vigour, weather resistance and attractive foliage are taken into consideration when selecting parents, although it does not follow that because both parents have these excellent qualities, the progeny will necessarily inherit them. Very often the undesirable qualities tend to be dominant and reveal themselves in subsequent generations.

Having decided on the parents, it is usual to lift plants in the autumn and to pot them into 8-inch or 10-inch pots, according to their size, trimming the roots to fit into the pot. Sufficient heat

1

4

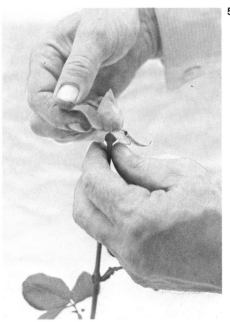

2

5

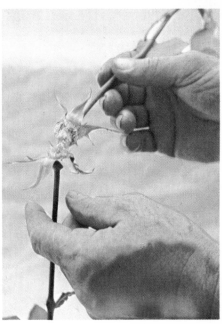

3

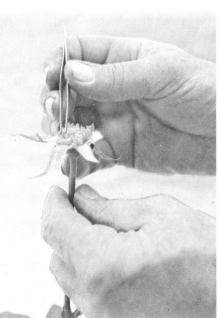

6

1 New varieties of Roses are produced by cross-pollination of selected parents. *Left* **The pollen parent and** *right* **the seed parent.**
2 Remove petals from the seed parent.
3 Remove anthers from the same flower, thus emasculating it.
4 and 5 The pollen is transferred from the pollen parent on to the stigma of the seed parent either by brush or by direct contact.
6 Label the parents, seed and pollen.

should be turned on to exclude frost, and flowers should be available towards the end of May when plenty of sunshine may reasonably be expected for cross-pollination, which should take place preferably on a sunny day. Not later than the half-open stage, the flower of the seed parent should have the petals pulled off one at a time, making sure that no small portion remains to set up decay. The flower should then be emasculated by removing all the anthers to prevent self-pollination. A small pair of nail scissors or tweezers may be used.

The stigma of the chosen seed parent remains, and if there are any insects about, this should be covered with a polythene or paper cap to prevent chance pollination. The stigma should be ready to receive the pollen by the following day, when it will be seen to be shiny and sticky. The best method of transferring the pollen of the male parent is directly from the anthers of the male flower,

holding the petals well back to ensure that the stigma receives a generous dusting of the pollen. After this, replace the cap at once and tie a small label to the footstalk of the seed parent, giving particulars of the cross, with the seed parent named first, e.g., 'Ena Harkness' x 'Margaret'. If all goes well the pollen will germinate and pollen tubes will grow down to the ovary inside the seed pod, there fertilising the ovum in the ovule to form an embryo. The seed pod will swell and begin to change colour in the autumn, when it should be cut off with a couple of inches of footstalk for after-ripening. This involves storing the pods in a mixture of moist peat and sand for at least three months, usually outside in a mouse-proof container.

By about February the fleshy part of the seed pod will have rotted, and the seeds can be separated easily by rubbing the pods between the palms of the hands. The seeds may be tested in water for

viability, those that sink, the 'sinkers', normally being regarded as fertile, and those that float, the 'floaters', being considered unlikely to germinate. The sinkers should be sown straight away in John Innes potting compost No 1, in pots, pans or boxes, ½ inch deep and 1 inch apart each way. The surface should be firmed with a piece of flat board and a good sprinkling of coarse sharp sand applied to discourage moss. A watering through a fine rose completes the operation. A temperature of 55° to 60°F (13–16 C) is suitable and better than a higher temperature. Germination will be irregular and the first seedlings are usually through in about six weeks. Some seeds may remain dormant until the second season or even later.

It is usual to pot up the seedlings into individual thumb pots when the first true leaf has developed, and to grow them on under glass until they flower. Many will be discarded at this stage, but a few may show some promise, either in colour or fragrance. The most promising seedlings are usually budded on small rootstocks outside, and it is only after being grown in this way for several seasons that the merits and faults of a seedling can be accurately assessed.

Exhibiting The rose is not always as easy as other flowers for exhibiting, as it must conform to show standards for but a very short time in hot weather. Pruning should be undertaken towards the end of March for a show in the latter part of June. In the specimen bloom classes, large flowers of good form, young and fresh, with firm petals of thick substance, are necessary. The colour should be rich and typical and the centre conical or spiral, high pointed, with two rows of outside petals reflexing to form a background. The petals should be free from insect holes and other blemishes; flowers with split, quartered or confused centres are useless for showing. In classes for 'decorative' roses size is less important, but brilliance of colour, freshness, perfection of form (HT) or truss (floribunda) are required, as well as tasteful and pleasing arrangement and healthy foliage.

Pruning, feeding, spraying and disbudding will have been attended to at the proper time. Preparation immediately prior to the show will start in earnest three days before, when tying and shading of the promising buds may be started (this is not desirable for the 'decorative' classes). Tying involves encircling opening buds with a length of thick soft wool placed inside the outside

1 The popular Rose 'Masquerade' is a hybrid. Its parentage is 'Goldilocks' x 'Holiday'.
2 Like all plants grown for showing, exhibition Roses must be given extra care, and the growths thinned.
3 Spraying is of utmost importance when growing Roses for exhibition.

row of petals, two-thirds of the way down from the point of the bud and drawing it firm with a double loop. The object is to restrict the expansion of the petals laterally in the hope that they will develop with greater length. Buds are at the right stage when the sepals have curled back and the outside row of petals is just separating from the hard centre. The petals should be dry at the time and a shade must be placed over the bud immediately for protection.

Flowers should be cut, allowing plenty of spares, either the evening before or very early on the show day. Each stem should be examined for insect pests, the prickles removed from the lower part, the bottom inch or so split and the leaves washed under running water. The bloom must be tested by removing the tie carefully and replacing it if the centre holds. Slightly damaged petals may be trimmed with nail scissors. Trusses of floribunda and other cluster roses may need tidying by removing faded flowers, including their footstalks. As many fresh young flowers as possible should be open in each truss.

All blooms intended for showing should have the stems immersed in water up to their necks for several hours beforehand in a cool place. The show schedule should be studied and if your own containers are permitted, these should be washed out in advance and rushes or coarse grass obtained for packing vases to facilitate arrangement. Florist's wire may be obtained for wiring of stems with weak necks, which is permissible.

For a local show roses may be transported in buckets. Entries are usually confined to vase and bowl classes nowadays. Equipment needed will include a sharp knife, secateurs, florist's

Roses exhibited at a show. Presentation is important and the show schedule rules must be followed closely.

wire, a soft camel's-hair brush, nail scissors, bowls and vases, a pen and packing material. Ample time should be allowed for staging. All vases are better packed loosely with rushes or grass; trim the packing flush with the rim and select the appropriate blooms.

In arranging three stems in a vase an inverted triangle is best, using the largest bloom for the base. For a vase with six stems of flowers, three levels— with two blooms in the highest, three in the middle and one in the lowest—are most effective. Any leaves below the waterline should be removed. The entry card is placed face downwards against the vase and the variety names shown on a separate card. Leave any ties in position until shortly before judging time. Where there is no background bowl classes usually require an all-round effect. Otherwise a frontal effect is best. Always select the brightest colours for the bowl, avoiding delicate shades except to separate the strong colours. The top of the bowl or grill should be hidden by the foliage and the stems so arranged that the flowers face in several directions and are on different levels, with pleasing colour contrasts.

Shortly before judging time carefully remove all ties from specimen blooms, taking care not to tear any petals. The centre should remain intact—if any fly open, revealing the anthers, they must be replaced. No blown bloom, nor any left tied, will score points. Assuming the centre holds, using the camel's-hair brush, the other petals should be pressed gently outwards and downwards, at the same time placing the middle finger of

the free hand behind each, so as to ensure a symmetrical outline.

Rose breeders' rights
In the same way that authors and song-writers may hold the copyright on their work, it is now legally permissible for those who raise or discover new roses to obtain exclusive rights over them. Breeders, or finders, of new plants are entitled to license growers, on payment of fees or royalties, to propagate and sell them, or to grow them for their cut flowers.

On the discovery of a new variety that is likely to become a commercial success, the best course is to apply immediately for a protective direction. This is much the same as 'patent applied for' protection, and is obtainable from: The Controller, Plant Variety Rights Office, Murray House, Vandon Street, London, SW1. An important condition attached to this preliminary step is that no plants or propagating material of any kind may be sold until full protection is given.

The protective direction safeguards the plant against 'piracy', a term aptly used to describe a practice still occasionally carried on in the horticultural trade. The fact that cuttings have even been stolen from plants while on display for the first time illustrates the importance of getting immediate protection.

After protective direction has been obtained, the next step is to get a better idea of the new plant's value. One way in which this is done is by submitting stock to the Royal Horticultural Society, Vincent Square, London, SW1. If it is considered of sufficient merit, stock of the plant will then be selected for trial at the RHS gardens as Wisley, Surrey. Plants can also be sent to the trials of the Royal National Rose Society. After an expert's assessment, it will be more clear whether it is worthwhile applying for full rights.

In order to do this, a pamphlet entitled *Guide to Plant Breeders' Rights* is available free from the Plant Variety Rights Office. The official requirements are that the variety must be clearly distinguishable by one or more important morphological, physiological, or other characteristic from all other varieties known at the time of application. The variety must be stable in its essential characteristics and remain true to description after repeated reproduction. And the variety must be sufficiently uniform in the particular features of its sexual reproduction.

When an application is made for full rights a name must be proposed that conforms with the *International Code of Nomenclature for Cultivated Plants*. Before rights are granted, the name of the new plant and a brief description is advertised in the *Plant Varieties and Seeds Gazette* to ensure that the name has not been used before and that the plant has not been sold under another name.

A Rose Gardener's Calendar

Successful rose growing depends to a large extent on careful planning. Roses require a considerable amount of attention and the various tasks must be carried out in a set sequence and at just the right time of the year.

A Rose Gardener's Calendar sets out clearly and concisely what needs to be done during each month, and how best to go about it. Climatic variations will affect the timing of the different treatments, but the essential thing is to be able to recognise when to act.

This guide will ensure that you do not omit any vital stage of rose care nor ruin your roses by giving them some treatment inappropriate for the season.

January

There are many passionately held theories about rose pruning and its timing. Of course much depends on soils and aspects, but most experts advocate gradual pruning from about the turn of the year through to March or April rather than a single, final pruning at any time of the year.

You can start to prune your roses on any January day when weather conditions are not too adverse.

First cut away all dead stems, all twiggy growth incapable of bringing forth a strong shoot and all side shoots growing into the centre of the bush. It is essential to allow light and air into the centre if strong, healthy growth is to be maintained. If there is time during the month continue the pruning process by cutting to about half their present length the remainder of the shoots, always to an eye pointing in the required direction.

You will probably have opportunities later on to hard prune. Even if you don't have, you will have done sufficient pruning to produce a fine show of blooms in the coming season and will, at the same time, have reduced the top

When Rose pruning, wear gloves and avoid windy weather; otherwise the whippy growths can be a hindrance.
1 The bush before it is pruned.
2 Dead and unwanted wood has been removed.
3 Cut back the leaders to an outward-facing bud a few inches above the ground level.
4 The finished job should look neat and leave a well-shaped skeleton to the bush. Light and air are important.

weight of the bushes to insure against rocking in high winds and the water-logging of roots.

You can plant roses—like all other shrubs—in January, provided the ground is not hard into frost or water-logged.

Newly planted bushes in medium to heavy soil should be cut down to within 6 inches or so of the soil, again to an outward-pointing eye. If they are planted in light or sandy soil it is best merely to tip them in their first year and to wait until they have made a good strong root system before being more drastic.

Roses like a slightly acid soil with a pH of about 6.0 or 6.5. If your soil is alkaline it can be improved with heavy dressings of compost, farmyard manure and peat. All these should be applied in the early spring, but as many farmers in January are overcrowded with manure this is a good time to obtain a supply.

February

Most of February work among roses will

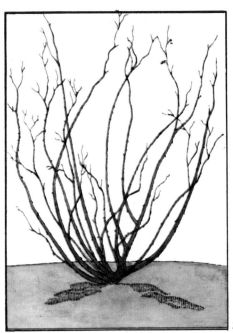

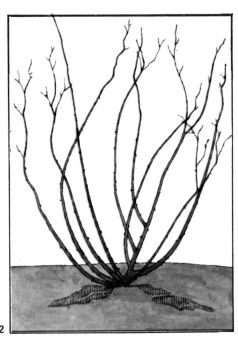

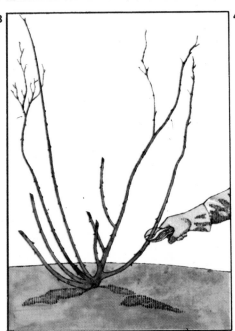

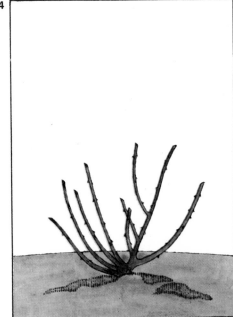

be concerned with planting and pruning. If the autumn and winter have been very wet, many autumn-purchased plants may still be heeled-in, awaiting sufficiently dry soil conditions. A friable soil is essential to successful planting. If the soil is a little too wet but not soggy, its condition can be made suitable by thoroughly incorporating some granulated peat.

Ideally, the rose bed should have been prepared several weeks earlier to allow the soil to consolidate. If this was not possible, it should be dug now.

Double digging in strips is best, the top soil from the second strip being thrown forward on top of the loosened subsoil of the first strip. The top soil from the first strip will be transferred to the opposite end of the bed to provide top soil for the final strip. By this method the fertile top soil is kept on the surface.

As much humus as can be spared should be incorporated as the digging proceeds. Mix it well in. Do not leave it as a separate layer. Well-rotted animal manure is ideal. But granulated peat, spent hops, garden compost, old hay and straw, leafmould, old chopped turf, sacking and waste of vegetable origin generally will all rot down to form valuable humus.

Before planting is started, a planting mixture should be prepared, consisting of a large bucketful of moist granulated peat into which two handfuls of either meat and bonemeal or sterilised bonemeal have been mixed. A shallow hole is taken out in the prepared bed, not more than 6 inches deep and wide enough to accommodate the roots without bending them. Several handfuls of the planting mixture should be added and the plant stood in the hole to check correct planting depth (so that the budding point is just covered). More planting mixture is thrown over the roots, together with some fine soil. The plant should then be gently raised and lowered to eliminate any air pockets. Further soil is added and then firmed moderately with the feet, starting on the outside edge of the hole and working towards the centre to avoid upsetting the level of the plant. The hole should be filled, finishing off with an inch or so of loose soil or peat.

Any dead or obviously exhausted or twiggy wood should be removed from established plants to simplify pruning later in the month or early in March.

March

Rose planting should be completed if at all possible during March. When planting during this month it is normal practice to prune in the hand before doing so. Take care to cut away all weak, damaged and dead wood and cut back

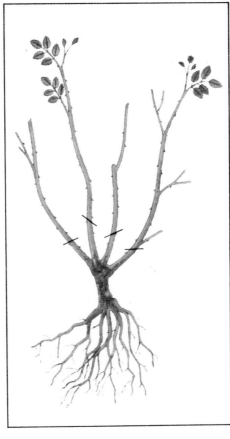

When a Rose is received from the nursery ready for planting it sometimes looks a straggly plant. When planting, allow plenty of room for the roots to be spread out and make them very firm. The growth should be cut right back to within a few inches of the ground. The position of the cuts is indicated.

the remaining sound wood to 3 or 4 eyes from the base.

The pruning of established roses should be undertaken early in the month before the new shoots become too long, as these will be on the upper half of the stems that will have to be cut away. Roses are best pruned when they are dormant and the dormant period varies from year to year according to severity of the winter. After a period of frosts or heavy snow it may be that the roses will still be dormant early in March but normally they should have started into new growth.

There is considerable variation in pruning methods depending partly on the requirements of the grower. Is he, for example, interested mainly in exhibition roses or in general garden display? The various main groups of roses call for various pruning methods and the type of soil on which roses are growing is also a differential factor.

Really hard pruning, which used to be widely practised for exhibition and formal bedding, is no longer considered essential with modern varieties. Many of them, particularly in shades of yellow, resent hard pruning that may result in

sparse flowering and split blooms. Most hybrid teas in shades of yellow, apricot, orange and flame give better results from moderate pruning.

There are certain preliminary operations common to all groups and to all methods of pruning. All dead, dying, badly diseased, damaged, thin, twiggy and unripe wood must first of all be cut away. So should any badly placed shoots, that is, those crossing other shoots or growing inwards to the centre of the plant, which should be kept open. When pruning, a sharp pair of secateurs should be used and all cuts should be made on the slant just above an outward facing eye, which is a dormant shoot bud.

Having removed the superfluous wood, you will get a better idea of the healthy wood that remains and needs to be shortened. This is explained below.

Hybrid Teas
This type may be pruned by one of three methods: *Light pruning* This involves cutting back any basal shoots of the previous season to just above the first or second outward-pointing eye below the footstalks of the old flowers. Laterals from older wood should be cut back by about a third of their length. The system is recommended for use on very hungry soils. Mulching the surface of the beds with organic matter is also advisable. *Moderate pruning* For garden display and the provision of cut flowers for the house, this method gives good results on most soils. It involves shortening growths made during the previous season by about half—rather more than this if they are slender and rather less if they are strong and sturdy. *Hard pruning* This method is more suited to the needs of the exhibitor of specimen blooms but it may also be preferred where formal beds on lawns require the plants to be kept compact and not to overhang the turf. Only the strongest of the healthy growths are retained. These are cut back to about 4 or 5 eyes from the base and any laterals or side shoots are restricted to 2 or 3 eyes. A rich soil and liberal feeding are recommended under this system to give good results over a lengthy period.

Floribundas
New basal shoots of the previous season should be left almost full length. Merely cut back to the first outward-pointing eye below the old footstalks. Laterals from 2-year-old wood should be cut back halfway and older wood which has not produced flowering laterals should be cut back hard to 3 eyes from the base.

Ramblers.
The category covers the wichuraianas and the multiflora ramblers. Those that renew themselves with new canes from the base every season should have all the old canes cut out after flowering and the new ones tied in to fill the space.

Others that do not renew themselves completely from the base should have as much of the old wood cut away as can be spared and all the new canes retained.

Climbers

The category includes modern recurrent climbers. Apart from removing old and twiggy wood and cutting back laterals to 3 eyes, little formal pruning is necessary. But horizontal training, to force the dormant eyes into growth along the length of the canes, is most important.

Shrub roses

These include Old Garden roses. Apart from the removal of twiggy wood and thinning out to avoid overcrowding, pruning is aimed at maintaining a symmetrical outline and avoiding bareness at the base. The aim is achieved by cutting back 1 or 2 main stems to within a foot or 15 inches of the soil as necessary. All prunings should be removed and burnt without delay.

April

In Scotland and the northern counties of England rose pruning will often not be completed before the middle of this month, although this is normally late for the southern counties and the West Country. The prunings should always be gathered and burnt, the resulting ashes being sprinkled over the surface of the beds. Provided they are kept quite dry, these ashes have a useful potash content.

After each bed or border has been pruned it is labour-saving to consider combining the pricking over of the trampled down surface with feeding and mulching. How this will be tackled depends very much on the type of feed available. For the fortunate gardener who has access to a supply of farmyard or stable manure, it may be sufficient if a dressing of sterilised bonemeal or meat and bonemeal is applied at the rate of 3 or 4 ounces per square yard, together with a lighter dressing of hoof and horn at 2 ounces per square yard. These organic fertilisers are slow-acting, and will gradually release their nutrients over many months.

The fertilisers should be pricked in with a border fork. Take care not to penetrate the soil more than an inch or so to avoid injuring valuable feeding roots. The mulch of animal manure is usually best applied when the soil has begun to warm up, which may not be before the early part of May, depending on the district where the garden is.

But the snag about leaving the mulch of animal manure until well into May is that, by this time, the new shoots following pruning will often be quite long and

very brittle. However careful one may be in spreading manure at this stage, many shoots are bound to be broken. On balance, therefore, mulching is probably best undertaken about the middle of April in the south and early in May in the north.

Most amateur rose growers are unable to obtain supplies of animal manures, or else they find the cost so high that they cannot use them every year. Where this

---

After the strong winter gales, all Rose tree stakes should now be tested and the ties should be adjusted wherever necessary.

is the case, it will still be necessary to use organic material as a surface mulch. This may take the form of granulated peat, fortified hop manure, leafmould, garden compost, spent mushroom compost (except on alkaline soil) or even old chopped hay and straw.

With these materials it is normally advisable to apply a complete rose fertiliser, and it is convenient to apply this to the surface of the soil immediately before applying the mulch. Tonks' Fertiliser is recommended as being well-balanced for nearly all soils. It is clean to handle, being a fine, odourless inorganic powder, and it should be sprinkled evenly over the soil surface at roughly 2 ounces every square yard. The mulch of organic matter needs to be not less than 2 inches thick to be effective in conserving moisture. If granulated peat is used, this should be moistened thoroughly before applying it to the surface of the soil. Otherwise it would absorb any rain or cause it to run off, in either case preventing it from reaching the roots.

Some gardeners may prefer to buy the ingredients and mix their own inorganic fertiliser. This does work out cheaper than purchasing complete fertilisers. The following formula will be found satisfactory on most soils:

	Parts by weight
Superphosphate of lime	16
Sulphate of potash	10
Sulphate of ammonia	5
Sulphate of magnesia	2
Sulphate of iron	2

The ingredients should be thoroughly mixed on the day when it is intended to apply them. All lumps should be crushed to a fine powder. Uneven mixing should be avoided as this, of course, is tantamount to varying the formula. The complete fertiliser should be sprinkled evenly over the surface of the soil, but it should not be allowed to fall on the wood or the leaves of the roses. If the weather is dry at the time of application, the fertiliser should be pricked in with a border fork and watered well. When feeding rose beds it is always well to bear in mind that nutrients can only be absorbed in solution, which is why it is essential that dry fertilisers should always be watered in.

April is a suitable time of year to test for firmness the stakes and ties of standard roses and the supports of pillar roses before the plants are in full leaf, when they will offer much greater wind resistance and be more vulnerable to gale damage.

In renewing the stakes of standards, ensure that they are long enough, when driven well home, to come right up into the head. This will provide greater support and allow two or three of the main stems forming the head to be tied to the stake for additional support in exposed gardens. The ties should preferably be of tarred twine or insulated cable for durability.

A strip of felt should be wrapped round the stake and the standard stem in figure-of-eight fashion before securing the tie to protect the bark of the stem against damage from chafing.

May

Early in the month it is advisable to go over rose bushes with a view to eliminating multiple shoots. Sometimes two or three shoots grow out from the eye just below the pruning cut. This may be due to frost having damaged the first shoot, so that two others appear, one on each side of the original one. Some varieties are very prone to producing multiple shoots even when there has been little or no frost damage. The correct procedure is to remove with the point of a penknife blade any shoots except the strongest one from each eye—otherwise there will be an over-crowded plant, and the shoots and flowers which develop from these eyes will not be of top quality. In addition, much thinning will prove necessary later on.

Pricking over and mulching the rose beds should be continued where this

Black spot, a fungus disease of roses, and 'shot hole' which can be caused by caterpillars. The remedy is to pick and spray with approved solutions.

was not completed in April. The soil should have warmed up quite appreciably by about the middle of the month and, if a supply of well-weathered soot happens to be available, it it useful to apply a dressing to the surface at the rate of 3–4 ounces per square yard. This will be of two-fold value. First, it contains sulphate of ammonia in small quantities and, secondly, by darkening the colour, it makes the soil a better medium for absorbing sun heat. As a consequence it should warm up quicker than lighter coloured soil.

It is important to keep a sharp lookout for insect pests during this month. Aphids (greenfly) are sure to be in evidence on the young shoots to some extent. They multiply very rapidly so it is wise to spray before they are very numerous. Any of the well-known contact sprays such as gamma BHC, malathion and derris should be effective in keeping down the number of this sap-sucking pest. It is always a good plan to spray again after an interval of about three days, as aphids have the ability to give birth to live young after they have been killed by insecticides. Care should be taken to spray the underside of the leaves as well as the upper

surface—otherwise large colonies of aphids will be missed. If a systemic spraying is preferred, formothion may be used.

During May, too, it becomes necessary to take action against other insect pests, including a wide range of caterpillars, the leaf-rolling saw fly, the larvae of the tortrix moth and the green capsid bug. Everybody will be familiar with the 'shot-holed' appearance of leaves infested with caterpillars, although a few of them eat the edges of the leaves, where damage may not be so noticeable. For nearly all biting and chewing insects such as caterpillars, the remedy, apart from hand-picking, is to spray the foliage with insecticide, which is poisonous to the pest. This soon dries on the surface of the leaf as a fine white deposit, which may need to be renewed after heavy and prolonged rain. Alternatively, a trichlorphon spray may be used with some effect.

The leaf-rolling sawfly is becoming more widespread as a rose pest. The adult female lays her eggs in the margins of the leaflets and at the same time injects an irritant which causes them to roll downwards and lengthwise. The larvae, on hatching, are able to feed on the inner tissue of the leaf without emerging. The rolling also reduces the leaf area by over fifty per cent and so interferes with the process of photosynthesis. Spraying with trichlorphon four or five times between mid-May and mid-June has produced encouraging results. Otherwise there is little one can do to combat this pest except to pick off and burn any rolled leaves immediately they are seen.

Sometimes leaves are noticed folded together unnaturally, or a leaf may be seen adhering to the footstalk or even to a flower bud. Other leaves may be folded upwards and inwards. If these

leaves are opened carefully, a small brownish maggot will usually be found. This is the larva of the tortrix moth, which can do a lot of damage in May and June. Hand picking of the folded leaves, after pressing them between the forefinger and thumb, and then burning them, is the only certain way of dealing with this pest as it is extremely difficult to reach the maggot with contact sprays, protected and folded as it is inside the leaf.

The green capsid bug is a sap sucker and may be seen in May and early June, probably mounted on a small terminal bud, sucking its sap. It is a bright metallic green in appearance, not unlike a very much enlarged aphid, but with long legs and extremely active. If disturbed it will either drop down to the soil or hide underneath a leaf. This pest injects a poison when it sucks the sap, so the young leaves which are attacked, apart from showing puncture holes, have a curiously distorted appearance. Buds which are attacked turn brown and shrivel up, so that the shoot gives the impression of being blind. Spraying several times before the end of May with gamma BHC is recommended. Make sure to thoroughly drench both surfaces of the leaves, the stems and any flower buds.

It may not be too early to start disbudding later in the month. To be effective this job must be tackled in the early stages. It is pointless to leave it until the unwanted buds are as large as peas. Where there are more than three buds on a stem of a hybrid tea, it is advisable to disbud in two stages, first reducing to three and then to one, with an interval of a few days between the two operations. Normally the centre bud of a cluster of three will be left to develop, as this is usually the most advanced.

When disbudding Hybrid Tea Roses, the buds need to be removed cleanly quite early in their development. This will encourage the formation of better and fewer blooms.

By removing the central bud of a truss on Floribunda Roses a better display can be had with more of the flowers open at the same time without being too overcrowded for good effect.

June

Disbudding will be one of the jobs requiring attention this month if the highest quality blooms are desired. It is not merely the hybrid teas which benefit from disbudding, contrary to popular belief. The removal of the centre bud of the truss in floribunda and modern shrub roses will often result in a better display, with more of the flowers open at the same time, but without these being overcrowded.

It will often happen during this month that soft side-shoots will start into growth before the terminal flower bud has opened. These side-shoots should be pinched out in the early stages while still soft. Otherwise they will divert the supply of sap from the main flower bud, which then will not develop its full potential. This form of de-shooting in the early stages is much more sensible than allowing the growths to mature and then cutting them back to relieve an over-crowded plant.

The grower who is interested in exhibiting his roses will wish to provide supplementary feeding during this month. There are numerous proprietary brands of 'complete' rose fertilisers and, properly used, these are satisfactory.

If home-made liquid feeds are preferred, these may be made by suspending a bag of animal manure in a water butt for a few days and then applying the liquid, diluted if necessary, so that it is never deeper in colour than a pale straw.

It is far better to apply two weak solutions of liquid manure than one of double strength, which may do more harm than good. Steps should always be taken to ensure that the soil is not dry when liquid manures are applied.

For inorganic stimulants, nitrate of potash—1 ounce dissolved in a gallon of soft water—is recommended, divided between two established bushes. Soot water may also be prepared by suspending a bag of soot in a butt of water, but as this is nitrogenous it should not be overdone, or soft growth may result which falls an easy prey to disease.

Mildew is the disease of roses which appears in all gardens, and spraying should be undertaken at the first sign of the powdery white or grey surface fungus appearing on the leaves. Under suitable conditions for its development mildew will spread rapidly. Preventive spraying is not the answer, but rather thorough spraying of both upper and under surfaces of the leaves at the first sign of infection.

Many growers use dinocap under the proprietary name of Karathane, but this is intended more for restricting the spread of the disease than for curing leaves which are already infected. Bouisol mixed with Volck is recom-mended by some growers; others find that 1 ounce of ordinary washing soda crystals dissolved in a gallon of soft water, with a little liquid soap added to act as a spreader, is as effective as most proprietary mildew sprays, as well as being considerably cheaper. Dryness at the roots seems to encourage an out-break, so any roses planted near walls or fences should be watered liberally during dry weather.

Rose growers who live in pure air districts which are troubled with black spot disease should start preventive spraying against attacks at the beginning of this month and continue every 10 days or so in really bad areas. The curious thing about this disease is that growers in industrial and heavily built-up areas are seldom troubled with black spot, as the amount of pollution in the atmosphere acts as a fungicide. In pure air districts, on the other hand, the spores of the fungus are able to develop unless regular preventive spraying is practised.

The only way to control black spot disease is by this regular spraying as, once the black spots have appeared on a leaf, that leaf cannot be saved. Maneb 80 and captan (e.g. Orthocide) are the most effective preparations, and both are sold as a fine wettable powder. As the disease attacks the older leaves at the base of the plant first, particular attention should be given to ensuring that these are thoroughly covered on both surfaces.

Continue to watch for insect pests, particularly caterpillars and the leaf-rolling sawfly, both of which can do a great deal of harm in quite a short time. Hand picking, if undertaken in the very early stages, can save a lot of trouble later.

During the second half of the month, at any rate in southern regions, there should be quite a colourful display from the hybrid tea bedding roses. Even farther north some of the climbing sports of the hybrid teas will be in bloom, as these normally flower about three weeks earlier than their bush counterparts. As the blooms fade they should be cut off with several inches of stem, just above a leaf, so that the dormant shoot bud at the junction of the leaf and stem can develop and replace the stem that has been removed. These sub-laterals, as they are called, will often carry a crop later in the season. On no account should seed pods be left to develop on any of the climbers, as this will prevent any further display.

When removing faded flowers from bedding roses it is best to cut back the stem to about half-way. Cutting back harder will cause a longer flowerless interval. Equally, if merely the old flower head is removed, the bush will tend to become overcrowded with many thin shoots. During the first season after planting, however, it is best to remove the flower with the footstalk, as every leaf is helpful in establishing a strong plant.

July

Many rose shows are held during the last week in June and the first week in July. As a matter of fact this fortnight represents the peak of the year for rose shows.

There is more to showing roses than going into the garden on the morning of the show, cutting whatever blooms may be available and arranging them in bowls or vases. The consistently success-ful exhibitor will almost live with his roses for the two or three days prior to the show. Even if he decides not to 'tie' young blooms in order to increase their size and length of petal, there is much to be done in arranging the conical bloom protectors to shield them on the plant from sun and rain and excessive heat.

The blooms are cut during the evening before the show and the stems are plunged immediately into cold water in deep containers, so that the water almost reaches the base of the bloom. Only those with perfect centres are suitable for exhibiting, i.e. where the centre forms a perfect cone or spiral, free from clefts or other irregularities. Most beginners tend to show their blooms well past their best, or even blown. Once the centre has opened out, revealing the anthers, the flower is useless for exhibiting as a specimen bloom, whatever its size.

When arranging a decorative bowl of roses, brightness and freshness are more important than size alone, especially when, as often happens, size goes hand in hand with insipid colours. There is scope in such an arrangement for skilful colour blending and contrast.

It is only by actually exhibiting his own roses that a gardener can compare his with the standard reached by other growers, and it may well act as a spur to further effort if his best blooms are not among the prize-winners. While experience in 'dressing' blooms will help to some extent in disguising faults, it cannot convert a bad flower into a good one.

The keen amateur will not be satisfied until he has tried his hand at budding and July is the month when this is normally undertaken. The rootstocks should have been planted in their budding quarters between January and mid-March, about 8 inches apart in the rows and 18 inches between the rows. The most popular rootstock is the seed-ling briar *(R. canina),* or one of its many selected strains, to ensure greater uniformity.

Many beginners go wrong because they take far too long over the job. It should be borne in mind that this is in the nature of a surgical operation on a plant, so that speed and cleanliness are essential to success. In budding, the cambium layer of the bud, i.e. the tissue between the wood and the bark, has to unite with that of the rootstock, and if this is allowed to dry out by taking too long over the job, the operation is bound to fail.

Apart from this, the essentials to success in budding are threefold: first, a really fresh bud in good condition; second, the removal of the wood behind the bud, without damaging the bud itself; third, the sap to be running freely in the rootstock, so that the bark will lift cleanly on both sides of the 'T' cut, without forcing or bruising.

In order to ensure the correct condition of the bud, a stem of the chosen variety on which the flower is just fading should be cut off just above the fourth leaf down from the flower. This will leave three buds on the stem—one at the junction of each leaf with the stem. The third one down from the bloom will normally be just right and maybe the second one also, depending on the variety. The leaves should be cut off apart from half an inch of the stalk, to facilitate handling the bud.

When removing the bud from the 'stick', as the stem is called, a really sharp budding knife should be used.

Starting half an inch above the bud, make a cut on the slant, gradually penetrating deeper behind the bud and then becoming shallower, so that the blade emerges half an inch beyond it. This severs a boat-shaped piece of bark with the bud and leaf stalk in the middle and a thin slice of wood behind. It is the removal of this wood without damaging the bud that causes most trouble, especially when too much wood has been left by cutting too deeply. The simplest method is to remove the wood in two operations. If the shield is held between the forefinger and thumb of one hand, with the thumbnail pressed hard against the wood behind the bud, and the top of the slice of wood above the bud is held between the forefinger and thumb of the other hand, a sudden sideways snatch will remove this wood without damaging the bud, which is protected by the thumbnail of the other hand. The shield of bark should then be reversed to remove the piece of wood below the bud in a similar manner. The base of the shield should then be trimmed straight across, prior to inserting it behind the flaps of bark raised in readiness on each side of the 'T' cut in the bark of the rootstock at soil level. As to whether moist raffia or the more modern rubber or plastic ties are to be preferred is a matter of opinion, but the beginner will probably find raffia easier to use. It

should be bound round the entire cut in puttee-fashion, but leaving the dormant bud itself exposed.

August

Any rootstocks not dealt with in July should be budded as early as possible this month, as there is a strong tendency for the sap to stop running sufficiently to give a good 'take', unless regular artificial watering is undertaken, in dry weather.

In general, standard stems, whether English briar or *rugosa*, should be budded early in the season to obtain a satisfactory 'take'. On the other hand, both cutting and seedling rootstocks of *R. polyantha multiflora* (syn. *R. multiflora japonica*) will usually bud reasonably well into August, as they continue to grow, even in dry weather. This rootstock has a very thin bark, so it will be necessary to tie the maiden growth to

Roses are budded in July.
1 The bud is removed with a sharp knife.
2 The scion is trimmed.
3 The pith is removed from the bud.
4 A T-shaped cut is made in the stock.
5 The bud is inserted into the cut.
6 The union is firmly bound with raffia.

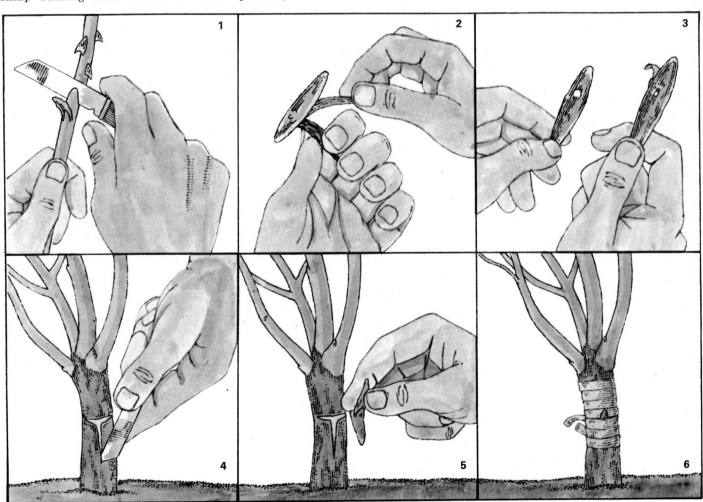

a short cane in the first season to avoid accidents from blowing about in high winds.

Spraying against black spot disease should continue at 10-day or fortnightly intervals, and if mildew is troublesome the bushes should be sprayed to keep the disease under control.

All the disagreeable insect pests do not usually prove unduly troublesome in August, but if aphids (greenfly) show signs of multiplying rapidly, a compatible insecticide could be added to the black spot spray to deal with them both in the same operation.

The second crop of hybrid teas and floribundas should be opening during the second half of the month, at least in the southern counties, as well as new shoots from the base. In general it is inadvisable to feed roses with nitrogenous fertilisers after the end of July, as these would encourage the production of soft wood which would probably become badly infected with mildew. On the other hand, it is recommended that the rose beds receive a dressing of sulphate of potash, at about 2 ounces to the square yard in mid-August, to encourage the ripening of the wood.

It is not too early to start cutting out the old wood which has flowered from established plants of Wichuraiana ramblers. A few of them which continue to bear flowers later in the season, such as 'Crimson Shower', should be left for another month or so, but most of them, especially those that flower early in the summer, such as 'Alberic Barbier', 'Albertine', 'Dr W. Van Fleet' and 'Francois Juranville', may now be tackled.

New basal shoots will already have appeared, and to avoid damaging these when drawing out the old canes, you should cut the latter into several pieces and pull them out separately. If there is doubt as to whether sufficient new canes will be forthcoming to replace the old wood, one or two of the flowered canes may be left to be on the safe side. All the new canes should be tied in as soon as possible, spacing them out evenly to avoid any overcrowding, which can encourage mildew. These rules also apply when cutting out the canes which have flowered from the heads of weeping standards.

In the case of the stiff-stemmed climbers, it is a wise plan to tie in the new canes as they grow and while they are still soft and pliable. This is the only really satisfactory way of training these canes in the right direction, as they harden in the desired position. By leaving the job over until the wood has hardened there is always a danger of the canes breaking off at soil level when they are being tied in, as some just will not bend.

Suckers from the rootstock must be dealt with as soon as possible after they appear above the soil. On no account

1 Fresh growth on Roses needs to be tied in now. Whippy growths of considerable length can be made during the summer and should be tied in now while they are still soft and manageable.
2 Similarly, young growth may have arisen from below the ground in the form of suckers. These must be severed.

should they be allowed to grow tall, as they will then flourish at the expense of the cultivated rose. Suckers can appear any time during the summer and autumn, but they are often fairly numerous in August. With a little practice it is quite simple to distinguish between suckers and basal shoots of the cultivated variety, as the leaves, prickles and stems are normally quite different. The leaves of suckers tend to comprise narrower and more numerous leaflets. These are pointed, whereas the leaflets of the cultivated rose are much broader and rounded. In the early stages the leaves of suckers are mostly green, whereas those of cultivated roses are often crimson, bronze and coppery tints. The prickles of suckers are numerous, narrow and pointed, whereas those of most cultivated roses are much broader, but fewer. The stems of suckers are usually pale green, compared with the red or bronze stems of young basal shoots of the rose.

Occasionally there may be some doubt as the the identity of a shoot in the early stages, and the only safe measure is to trace it carefully to its point of origin with the aid of a small trowel. A sucker will spring from either the root system or the main stem, below the budding point, whereas a true rose shoot can only emerge from the budding point or higher. It is important to remove all suckers by tracing them to the point from which they emerge on the roots or main stem and then pulling them off. Cutting will only encourage them to multiply.

Suckers will also sometimes appear on the stems of standard roses, and may even develop from the stem between the two budding points, so that the sucker becomes entangled with the head. It is necessary to pull it off before it attains any size, when it will be much more difficult to remove.

Before you go on holiday remove all flowers from your roses. These will only have died and may have set seed pods before your return. If the weather is dry, climbers against walls or tall fences should be given a really thorough soaking—say three large bucketsful per specimen.

September

Weeding will take up much time in a country district, especially where open fields are adjacent to the garden. The only satisfactory way of coping with this problem is to keep the weeds under control while they are still small. In a wet season, however, this is extremely difficult in a large garden. Weedkillers based on paraquat may be tried, although it is not claimed that these will kill perennial weeds, which are the ones that give the most trouble in a permanent planting, such as a rose bed. In applying the weedkiller it is best to use a special dribble bar which will fit on a plastic watering can. As it is non-selective in its action, this weedkiller must not fall on any soft young growth springing from the base of the roses.

Spraying to control black spot in pure air districts should be continued well into the autumn, as this is when the disease can spread very rapidly. Always see that the base of the plant is sprayed really thoroughly, as the disease attacks the oldest leaves first. Heavy autumn rains will wash much of the protective spray off the foliage so it may be necessary to spray more frequently than in summer to give adequate protection.

It will still be desirable to remove dead blooms, which can spoil the whole effect if left on the plants, but at this time there is no point in cutting the stem back half-way. It is sufficient merely to remove the dead flower with it attached to a piece of the footstalk.

Early frosts may occur in the first week of October, so some disbudding is strongly recommended. Remove all small buds which are unlikely to be open by then. It is far better to mature about one-third of the buds than to have all of them frosted before they can open.

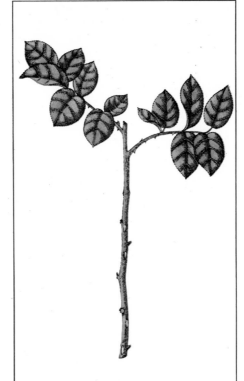

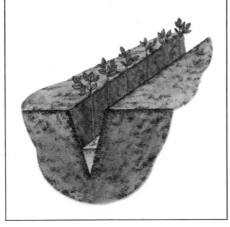

Above **Rose cuttings are made from ripened wood, about 9 inches long. First the tip is removed and then a straight cut is made at the base.** *Below* **The cuttings are inserted in a grip out of doors.**

Any extra long shoots which appear on bedding roses should be shortened about the end of the month. Autumn gales tug at these long shoots, causing great strain on the roots. The shoots, which are battered against the thorns of adjacent growths, become lacerated and the soil around the base of the plant is loosened, causing a cavity in which water may freeze. This will cause the roots to break.

It is a sound plan to examine all forms of support in late September, before the autumn gales start in earnest. In really exposed gardens windbreaks may be necessary, and tripods will be a sounder proposition than single upright pillars.

The edges of beds cut in lawns should continue to be trimmed, to set off the autumn display of roses which, in a well-maintained garden, will often almost equal the early summer display.

Towards the end of the month cuttings may be taken of the more vigorous groups of roses. It is questionable whether this is worth while with most of the hybrid teas in shades of yellow, apricot, orange, flame and bicolours, but many of the floribundas will root quite easily. Of course, groups like the Wichuraiana ramblers and many of the shrub roses will grow vigorously on their own roots, and may also be propagated from layers. The miniature roses are usually propagated from cuttings in order to retain their dwarf habit of growth.

Cuttings, except of miniature roses, should be about 9 inches long and prepared from well-ripened wood of the current season's growth. The wood produced immediately following spring pruning is best, as it is sure to be ripe enough. When preparing the cuttings the pithy growing tip should be rejected. All leaves except the top two should be removed and a cross-cut made to form the base of the cutting just below an eye or dormant shoot bud. The bottom inch of each cutting may be dipped in water and then in hormone rooting powder to hasten root formation.

A V-trench should be taken out in a sheltered part of the garden, making it about 6 inches deep and mixing coarse sand and moist granulated peat into the soil forming the base. The cuttings should be spaced about 4 inches apart and the soil firmed moderately as the trench is filled in. Only the top 3 inches of the cuttings will be above soil level, and it will help to conserve moisture if the surface is covered with granulated peat to a depth of 2 inches. The cuttings should then remain undisturbed for at least a year, and should never be allowed to dry out.

When cuttings of the miniature roses are taken they have, of necessity, to be very much shorter and are more conveniently inserted round the circumference of a 4- or 5-inch pot filled with a porous potting compost. Because of their diminutive size they are perhaps more conveniently kept in a cold frame or a cool greenhouse.

Advantage may be taken of any fairly flexible long shoot of a climbing or shrub rose to increase it by layering. Here the technique consists of making a slit in the lower side of the shoot, so that when it is bent to the soil level the slit opens to form a tongue, which is usually anchored to the soil by a wooden peg and a small pebble inserted in the tongue to keep it open. By heaping gritty soil over the tongue, rooting is encouraged, but the shoot is not severed from the parent plant until it is seen, by the new growth emerging from the point of pegging down, that the roots are active and able to support the shoot independently.

October

If no severe frosts occur, roses will continue to flower well into this month, and there is often a surprisingly good display. Nevertheless, it is advisable to bear in mind that sharp frosts may occur at any time, and there is no point in leaving flower buds to be ruined. Any which are showing colour, with the sepals separated from the bud, may be cut at this stage for opening indoors.

October is a time when autumn gales may be expected, and it is sound practice to shorten any extra-long growths and to tie-in to their supports the long new canes on climbing and rambling types. If this is not done the winds will not only damage the long canes, but will injure nearby shoots, too. The stakes and ties of all standard and half-standard roses, as well as those of weeping standards, should also be tested and renewed as required, without waiting for the plant to be blown over.

Spraying against black spot and powdery mildew will still be necessary, to avoid a build-up of these diseases which might well carry them over into the following season. As long as the plants carry plenty of foliage they will need protection against black spot at any rate, and with rain likely to be heavier or more frequent now, it is important to ensure that the spray is renewed whenever it is washed off.

Preparation of the ground for autumn planting should begin soon. The planting itself may be undertaken later in the month, if the plants can be obtained so early from the rose nursery. Most rose specialists like to defer lifting until some natural defoliation has taken place.

Nowadays, however, new chemical defoliants are sometimes used, and the plants are 'topped' at the nursery to remove the soft autumn growth. From the customer's point of view it is better to have a hard-wooded, well-ripened plant of moderate size than a larger one comprising mainly sappy, immature wood which may not survive the winter frosts.

In preparing the site for rose planting, one should be chosen which has not grown roses at all in recent years—otherwise, the soil is likely to be 'rose-sick' and new plants will not thrive. The best plan is to double-dig the bed, making sure that the fertile top-spit remains at the top and the less fertile second-spit remains underneath.

It is quite easy to ensure this if the bed is divided into strips, about 1–8 inches wide, and the top soil from the first strip

is carried to the opposite end of the bed to be used for filling up the final strip. The sub-soil of the first strip is loosened then manure (well-rotted), compost and old chopped turf should be added.

The top soil from the second strip is then used to fill up the first strip. The sub-soil of the second strip is loosened and manure and compost are added and the top soil from the third strip used to fill up, and so on for the whole of the bed.

Additional humus-forming material, such as moist granulated peat, old hay and clean straw and such vegetable waste may be thoroughly forked in as the preparation of the bed proceeds—it should not be left as a sandwich between the top-spit and the sub-soil.

On shallow chalk soils it will be necessary to remove some of the chalk, so that there is at least 18 inches of reasonably good soil above the solid chalk. Skimping this job now will probably result in a great deal of trouble later on from lime-induced chlorosis, a disease caused by iron deficiency due to the locking up of the iron which forms an insoluble compound with the chalk and causes yellowing of the leaves and poor growth. On hungry, sandy soils every effort should be made to improve their moisture-retaining properties. This can be achieved by burying old turf (grass side downwards), leafmould, old sacks, carpets and rugs cut up into strips, old clothes, newspapers and

Any Rose buds that are showing colour between the sepals should be cut and put in water to open indoors. If they are left on the bush they will very probably be ruined by early frosts.

anything else that will absorb and retain moisture.

Care should always be taken to make sure that these materials are thoroughly moist before the top soil is replaced.

On heavy clay the problem will be to open up the soil so that it does not become a sticky, impervious mass in wet weather and baked to a brick-like hardness, with wide cracks, during dry spells.

There are a number of easy methods of breaking down heavy clay. Ridging to expose the maximum surface area to the action of severe frosts is the oldest method, and this can be supplemented by forking in generous quantities of compost, granulated peat and strawy stable manure, if the latter is available. It should be emphasised that this is a gradual process, extending over many seasons. For quicker results either hydrated lime or gypsum (sulphate of lime) may be used. A heavy dressing, normally applied to the sub-soil during the process of double-digging (up to 2 lb per square yard on a very heavy clay) will materially assist in breaking up the clay and making it more porous.

After the new site has been thoroughly prepared, several weeks should be allowed for the soil to settle and consolidate before attempting to plant. In areas of high rainfall it is a good plan to cover the bed with a large tarpaulin sheet. This will ensure that the soil is not too wet when the plants are delivered at the end of the month or in early November.

Where maiden plants budded earlier are available, it is often convenient to transplant these from the nursery rows to their permanent beds during October, before the November rains have made the soil too soggy for planting. If these maiden plants should still be in full leaf, due to a mild autumn, it is wise to cut off all the leaves and flower buds before transplanting, to prevent possible shrivelling of the wood from excessive transpiration

November

This is the earliest month that the rose specialists can usually hope to dispatch the plants. In the average season the wood is not ripe enough for lifting with complete safety much before November.

Nearly all roses are now dispatched in multi-ply paper sacks, and while these are strong enough to protect the plants from damage in transit they are not really frost-resistant. So the roses should be unpacked as soon as possible. If there should be a frost when the package is received it should be placed in an unheated, but frost-proof shed, where the plants will come to no harm for a few days. As soon as this can be done they should be removed from the package and sprinkled liberally with water. If the roots are dry they should be stood in tepid water for several hours.

There is quite a wide variation between different nurseries in the amount of trimming undertaken before dispatch. The larger rose specialists remove the soft growth from the tops before lifting mechanically. Some, but not all, remove the leaves, but usually there are many of these still on the plants dispatched in November. All of these leaves and any flower buds or soft, sappy young shoots should be cut off as soon as possible. If the leaves are allowed to remain they may lead to shrivelling of the stems from loss of moisture due to transpiration. In addition, any broken stems or roots should be cut away cleanly just beyond the damage.

If it should happen that the consignment is delayed in transit it may be that the stems will be shrivelled when the package is opened. It is a waste of time planting with the stems in this condition.

The most effective treatment is to dig a fairly deep trench, lay the plants horizontally at the bottom and then cover them completely, both roots and stems, with 6 inches of soil, firming this so that there is complete contact between soil and stems.

If the soil in the trench is at all dry the trench should be watered well after burying the plants. After a week or ten days the plants should be unearthed and by then the wood should have plumped up, allowing the roses to be planted normally.

The correct planting depth is when the budding point, i.e. the swollen part from which the top growth emerges, is just covered with not more than an inch of soil. Standard roses should always be planted as shallowly as possible, so that the top roots are only just covered. A stout stake should be driven home before the roots are covered to avoid possible injury. Dig a hole large enough to take the roots when spread out to their maximum—they should never be bent round to fit into too small a hole.

Finally, plenty of moist granulated peat, to which a little bonemeal has been added, should be mixed with the soil in direct contact with the root system and thoroughly firmed to ensure proper contact between roots and soil.

December

Rose planting should be continued if the weather and soil conditions are suitable. If plants are received when the soil is too wet for planting, they should be 'heeled in' until the soil is friable enough for permanent planting. A trench should be dug in a sheltered part of the garden and the plants laid in singly, at an angle of 45 degrees.

When planting a Rose standard stake it first and plant it to the correct depth, that is so that the swollen union is just covered with soil. You should always ensure that the roots are well spread out.

The roots of the plant and the lower part of the stems should be covered with soil, or a mixture of soil and peat if the soil is very heavy, and firmed moderately. Care should be taken to see that the labels are well above soil level, and the plants should be spaced out so that one may be removed without disturbing its neighbours.

When properly 'heeled in' rose plants will come to no harm, even if planting in their permanent quarters has to be deferred until March.

All fallen rose leaves should be raked up from the surface of the beds and burnt. This is particularly important when severe attacks of rust or black spot have occurred during the previous season.

To take a further precaution against the carry-over of disease to the following season it is a wise plan to spray the plants during this month with Bordeaux mixture or, alternatively, with copper sulphate, at a strength of 1 ounce per gallon of water. One gallon of the dilution is sufficient to spray the plants in an area of about 8 square yards. Copper sulphate in solution should only be mixed in a plastic container, it can corrode metals.

There is no reason why a start should not be made on the pruning of some groups, such as the hardy shrub roses, the Kordesii group, the Wichuraiana ramblers if these have not been dealt with earlier, or even some of the floribunda-shrub group. Dead wood may be cut out of roses belonging to any group as soon as it is noticed, as this wood can only harbour disease spores and cannot possibly benefit the plant. Many of the shrub roses will benefit by thinning out some of the twiggy wood and by cutting out completely any canes which have obviously become exhausted. These often show a yellowish tinge and do not carry any strong side-shoots.

In addition, it is useful at this time to look at the shape of shrub and hedging roses and to practise some judicious trimming to ensure a more symmetrical outline. This applies more particularly to large specimen bushes. Any dead or diseased wood and trimmings should be burnt as soon as possible.

When the ground is frozen is a good opportunity for barrowing soil, manure and compost, as it would be difficult to do this to any extent in mild weather without damaging the turf. Usually it is possible to push ahead with any reconstruction work at this time, such as the clearing out of old shrubberies, the preparation of new borders, the erection of pillars and rustic screens.

Pot roses which have been sunk up to their rims outside since June should be brought under glass during December and kept in cool conditions for a few weeks. They may be pruned hard back towards the end of the month for flowering at the end of April.

Planning a Rose Garden

Planning and design The hours of pleasure you'll find in a rose garden are the happy results of your care and labour in cultivation. Roses provide natural and lasting colour and effect and in the long run save work and expense. The planning of your garden is essentially a matter of personal choice, but there are some basic considerations and every landscape has its own special requirements.

A garden overcrowded with features is probably less satisfying and more difficult to maintain than one of quiet simplicity. Plan just a few focal points, such as a pool or a bower or a low wall. Take advantage of an attractive view by framing it in a hedge. Likewise, camouflage an offensive shed by setting tall bushes around it or minimise a slope by effective terracing. And don't forget that the garden design is governed more by the shape of your house than the shape of your plot. It's safest to draw up a plan of your site noting any permanent structures and trees, and then visualise the landscaping.

These general features of your garden will determine where you will want to place your rose beds. Roses are not difficult to position, provided they get

A lovely garden could be built around these two pleasant features: a quiet pool and a cool archway supporting some of the stronger-growing types of roses.

90

sun for most of the day with, ideally, a period of shade. Avoid any spot which is draughty, as between two buildings, or which is overhung by trees or where the roots of trees are running under the ground. You must then decide whether the layout is large enough to take roses grown in beds and borders on their own, or whether the roses must fit in with other plants in mixed borders. In a formal rose garden there are separate beds for individual varieties, whether of hybrid tea or floribunda type. These beds are cut in lawns with the possible inclusion of several standard or half standard roses of the same variety to give added height.

Although well-kept turf is the best setting for roses it involves a great deal of labour to maintain in first-class condition and it is always advisable to

have at least one dry path crossing the rose garden, so that barrowing can be done in wet weather without cutting up the turf. Crazy paving or formal stone paving slabs are best for this dry path, with cement run between the crazy paving stones to provide a firm surface and to reduce the labour of weeding. Normally rose beds about 5 feet wide are to be preferred to rose borders against a wall or fence, on the grounds of accessibility for weeding, pruning and cultivation generally. A bed of this width will accommodate three rows of plants, 18 inches between the rows with 1 foot at each side between the outside rows and the edge. This will be sufficient to

A bold and satisfactory effect is always obtained from Roses when varieties are planted in groups.

avoid an overhang with nearly all varieties, which would otherwise interfere with mowing and trimming the edges, if the setting is grass.

The shape of the rose beds is a matter for personal taste, but a simple design is normally best, and it involves less labour for maintenance. It should always be borne in mind that numerous small beds cut in a lawn, apart from looking fussy, require the edges trimming regularly and also slow down the operation of mowing the lawn.

Few amateurs can afford the space to have beds confined to one variety, but mixed beds should be selected carefully, and the varieties chosen for either tasteful colour blending or for similar habit of growth. Alternatively, the centre of the bed should be planted with a variety of taller growth and the perimeter with one of more compact habit. It is far better to plant six or more of the same variety in a group than to dot them about in ones and twos, and this holds good whether beds or borders are being planted.

In a rose border or a mixed border featuring roses and other plants, bold groups are essential for maximum display. In a deep rose border, the grading of groups of varieties according to height will be desirable, with the tallest at the back, although monotony may be avoided by breaking up the gradings with an occasional group of taller varieties running towards the front, or a single pillar or tripod with recurrent-flowering climbing roses about the middle.

Colour grouping with roses is again a matter of personal taste. Some people delight in the extreme contrast between a pure scarlet and a deep golden yellow, whereas others might find this garish, and prefer colour harmonies in blends of soft pink, apricot and orange shades. Some may prefer to group the same, or similar, colours together. The object of colour blending, of course, is to bring out the best in each colour by careful association of adjacent colours. Thus, white and orange-scarlet next to each other will emphasise, by contrast, the purity of the white and the brilliance of the orange-scarlet. On the other hand, orange-scarlet next to deep carmine pink would be an unhappy combination, as the blue in the carmine pink would look crude and harsh by contrast with the orange-scarlet.

As a general guide shades of yellow will associate well with shades of red. Orange, flame and apricot contrast well with dark crimson. Deep pink, especially carmine pink and cerise, is safest with cream, primrose yellow or white, and the same is true of lilac, lavender and mauve. These shades in roses are often dull in the garden and may need enlivening with bright yellow close by. Scarlet, orange-scarlet, crimson, deep pink and cerise are better separated from each other by using buffer groups of the soft pastel shades of cream, flesh, amber and off-white.

The question of whether to use other plants for carpeting rose beds often arises, bearing in mind that the roses do not normally provide much colour until June. Violas as ground cover or border plants add colour in the spring. Low growing plants, such as aubrieta, arabis and the 'mossy' saxifrages may also be used for edgings, but they will need shearing back after flowering. There is no reason either why shallow-rooted annuals should not be used, such as eschscholtzias, love-in-a-mist and night-scented stocks.

Slow growing conifers may also be used for effect. These have the advantage of being evergreens, and will improve the appearance of the rose garden, although the rank growers should be avoided. The Irish juniper, *Juniperus communis hibernica*, is excellent and takes up little space with its narrow, erect growth. The same is true of *Chamaecyparis lawsoniana columnaris glauca* in blue-grey, and the Irish yews, *Taxus baccata fastigiata*, and the golden *aurea*. Two very splendid slow-growing forms are *Chamaecyparis lawsoniana ellwoodii* and *fletcherii*. Both of these will remain below or about 5 feet in height for many years. Clematis may also be planted either by themselves or with recurrent flowering pillar roses, and will often be outstanding, introducing colours not found among roses. *Clematis jackmanii* in rich violet-purple will make a splendid pillar when planted with roses 'New Dawn' or 'Aloha'.

You can vary the appearance of your garden by combining several varieties of other plants which bloom at different times. Or a few well-placed herb beds or borders would be a nice touch.

Roses as hedges These may be divided into two groups, internal and boundary hedges. Internal hedges need not be as tall as boundary hedges and may include vigorous hybrid tea type roses, lightly pruned, such as 'Peace', 'Eden Rose', 'Tahiti', 'Rose Gaujard', 'Buccaneer', 'President H. Hoover', 'Super Star', 'Golden Masterpiece', 'Gold Crown', and the new blood-red 'Uncle Walter'. It does not matter about them being gappy at the base as they are not functional. The more upright growers should be planted fairly close together, and a staggered double row with the trees about 18 inches apart in each direction will help them to grow together quickly.

To provide a high focal point for your garden, many of the more vigorous roses may be grown against pillars, either single posts or tripods.

Strong-growing floribunda roses are also suitable and perhaps the best of all for a continuous display of colour. Such varieties as 'Queen Elizabeth', 'Frensham', 'Faust', 'Honeymoon', 'Lubeck', 'Daily Sketch', 'Shepherd's Delight', 'Sweet Repose' and 'Ama' will make a lovely mass display and seldom be without colour from June to October. There are too, the modern shrub roses, hardly less floriferous than the floribundas, which they closely resemble in flower type, but which have even stronger growth. Such excellent examples as 'Elmshorn', 'Dorothy Wheatcroft', 'Fred Loads', 'Lavender Lassie', 'First Choice', 'Nymphenburg' and 'Chinatown' offer a wide choice of colour.

Those who find an appeal in the soft, refined colouring of the old Pemberton hybrid musks may derive great pleasure from a hedge of such favourites as 'Penelope', 'Prosperity', 'Moonlight', 'Felicia', 'Cornelia', 'Vanity' and 'Thisbe', as well as enjoying their distinctive fragrance. All varieties mentioned for internal hedges are recurrent flowering.

1 Rose 'Pink Supreme' used to form a decorative hedge in a Rose garden.
2 One of the old Pemberton Hybrid Musk Roses, 'Penelope' forms a good hedge.

For boundary hedges rather different qualities are required. If animals have to be discouraged, very strong growers with thorny wood, such as the hybrid rugosa 'Conrad F. Meyer', are very useful, as are most of the hybrid rugosas, including 'Blanc Double de Coubert', 'Sarah van Fleet', R. rugosa rubra and R. rugosa alba. While not as recurrent flowering as modern types, they have the attraction of brilliant scarlet tomato-like hips in the autumn and leaves which then change colour to an attractive gold and russet and crimson shades. To obtain plenty of colour in a boundary hedge it may be necessary to introduce some of the modern recurrent flowering climbers and shrub roses. 'Queen Elizabeth' will easily reach a height of 7 feet. Unfortunately most of the really thorny varieties bear their flowers early in the season and are not reliably recurrent.

Some of the species and hybrids of species would also be very useful as boundary hedges because of their thorns. These include 'Nevada', pale creamy-white, tinted pink; 'Fritz Nobis', flesh pink shaded salmon; 'Frühlingsgold' clear yellow; 'Frühlingsmorgen', deep pink, with yellow centre; R. moyesii. blood red, followed by bottle-shaped scarlet hips; and R. sericea pteracantha (syn. R. omeiensis pteracantha) with huge, broad translucent ruby-red thorns on young red wood, and small white flowers.

The wichuraiana rambler roses may be interplanted with those of more rigid, upright growth in boundary hedges. They mostly have lax canes which need

some support. This may take the form of a post and wire fence, individual uprights or adjacent shrub roses of erect habit. They mostly have a short but glorious burst of colour in June and July. 'Alberic Barbier', 'Emily Gray', François Juranville' and 'Sanders' White' are four with a particular appeal because, even when they are not in flower, the glistening foliage is beautiful in itself and retained for much of the winter.

Finally, when considering roses as hedges, the claims of the modern recurrent-flowering pillar roses should not be overlooked. These could be alternated with the hybrid wichuraianas to give colour over a longer season. Such varieties as 'Joseph's Coat', yellow, orange and red; 'Maigold', coppery yellow; 'Golden Showers', medium yellow; 'Danse du Feu', orange-scarlet; 'Bantry Bay', rose pink; 'Pink Perpétué', rose pink with carmine pink reverse; 'New Dawn', flesh pink and 'Schoolgirl', apricot-orange; are all highly recommended, and give an extra dimension to your garden planning. They need little pruning and have a high proportion of flowers to wood.

Index

Numbers in italics indicate an illustration, and a, b or c after a number indicates the column on the page where the material is to be found.